FOR A EUROPEAN AWAKENING

FOR A

EUROPEAN AWAKENING

NATURE, EXCELLENCE, BEAUTY

ESSAYS BY

PHILIPPE CONRAD • RÉMY SOULIÉ • HENRI LEVAVASSEUR •
JEAN-PHILIPPE ANTONI • JEAN-FRANÇOIS GAUTIER • THIBAUD
CASSEL • ALIX MARMIN • JEAN-YVES LE GALLOU • GUILLAUME
TRAVERS • OLIVIER EICHENLAUB • ANNE-LAURE BLANC • PAUL
ÉPARVIER • GRÉGOIRE GAMBIER • ALAIN DE BENOIST

ARKTOS
LONDON 2023

ΛRKTOS

⊕ Arktos.com 𝐟 fb.com/Arktos ◉ @arktosmedia ⊙ arktosmedia

ISBN

978-1-915755-30-8 (Paperback)
978-1-915755-31-5 (Hardback)
978-1-915755-32-2 (Ebook)

Translation
Roger Adwan

Editing
Jason Rogers

Layout & Cover
Tor Westman

CONTENTS

III. Beauty as Our Horizon

IV. Conclusion

᠀

'WHERE DANGER LIES, SALVATION ALSO GROWS.'

BY PHILIPPE CONRAD[1]

I T WAS BY deliberately taking his own life seven years ago that Dominique Venner meant to warn us of the fatal course which Europe, our own Europe, was pursuing. At the time, many historians and essayists had, for several decades, been analysing the civilisational crisis witnessed today by our contemporaries. Beyond the mutations befalling the economy and the setbacks stemming from a globalisation that was initially presented as both inevitable and inexorably favourable, it is with a genuine anthropological revolution, one that calls into question all the traditional fundamentals of our very society, that Europeans are now faced at the beginning of the 21st century.

Endowed with an ancient, mediaeval heritage that allowed it to become a privileged space harbouring an unequalled sort of civilisation, Europe was the first to accomplish, from the 16th century onwards, the breaking-down of global barriers that went hand in hand with the dawning of modernity, which allowed it to impose its hegemony upon the entire world. Its scientific revolutions and industrial take-off are what enabled it to completely dominate, a little more than a century ago, the whole of our planet, as it found itself in a position to impose

---

1 · TN: Born on 29 March 1945, Philippe Conrad is a French essayist.

its own representations and models upon the rest. Having reached its peak at the start of the previous century, it would then plummet, from 1914 to 1945, into a suicidal 'thirty years' war', with the Hellenist Albert Thibaudet drawing an analogy between the latter's initial phase and the Peloponnesian War, a war which resulted in the ruin of the world of Greek cities during the 5th century B.C. In terms of power, the 'dark twentieth century' thus bore witness to the shifting of the world's centre of gravity towards North America, itself the bearer of a new civilisational model originally inspired by Wilsonian universalism and liberal delusions. The weakening that resulted from the ruin of the old European world was exacerbated further — despite the reassuring guarantees seemingly offered by technological and economic progress during the second half of the previous century — by the cultural revolution that took place in the 1960s and whose caricatural expression was our great masquerade of 1968. The time had thus come for a methodical 'deconstruction' of our identities and heritages, all in the name of the desired advent of a 'borderless' world in which the hedonistic individualism of the Enlightenment and its developments were henceforth bound to condemn any form of attachment to one's historical roots, as well as all familial or national determinism and an entire culture denounced for acting as the very reflection of class (or, today, perhaps even racial) domination. In the world dreamt up by the likes of Jacques Attali[2] and George Soros, the 'nomadic' individual of future 'open societies' will be limited to his *homo economicus* and *homo festivus* functions and defined as a producer-consumer that shall be rewarded for his docility by being granted generalised access to both 'happiness' and leisure civilisation, in a world that shall hardly leave any room for one's spiritual aspirations, personal reflection or the culture of an intellectual tradition that has made us who we are. The globalist liberal project, which was devised overseas and passed on to Brussels by a European Union that has little to do with the genuine

---

2   TN: Jacques Attali is a French author, political adviser, civil servant, and economic and social theorist.

Europe whose awakening we so desire, does, however, seem rather hard to implement. When one considers the end of the USSR and the Soviet bloc thirty years ago, China's spectacular rise to power, the Islamic awakening that surfaced at the turn of the 1980s, the return of previously sidelined actors to the global stage and the emergence of new poles of power, all of it seems to shatter any and all hopes of multilateralism and global government for a long time to come. It is therefore all too clear that *realpolitik* is reclaiming its rightful place, a fact that the Europe of Brussels has no intention of taking into account.

We have thus entered the era of perils. Today, the frantic race towards continuous economic growth comes across as a catastrophically evasive attitude on the economic, social and ecological front. The cultural transmission crisis gives birth to entire generations of amnesiacs that remain quite incapable of analysing the causes of the disaster currently in progress. Societies dominated by globalised metropolises have become, in the eyes of most of their members, uninhabitable spaces, and virtually everywhere, uncontrolled population flows have realised the visions which the late Jean Raspail[3] detailed almost fifty years ago in his prophetic work entitled *Le Camp des Saints*.[4] At a time when European peoples are faced with the threat of the Great Replacement, it is the danger of the Great Erasure of their respective memories which now represents the main challenge of the struggles to come. The relinquishment of traditional humanities and the lack of space dedicated to history and to the transmission of our literary and artistic heritage are very revealing indeed when it comes to current trends...

Faced with this alarming situation, we have no choice but to fight a merciless cultural battle, one whose outcome will determine the future; for should we be unfortunate enough to lose, we would risk finding ourselves confronted with situations that are much more serious than

3   TN: Jean Raspail was a French writer, traveller and explorer whose numerous books centred around historical figures, exploration and indigenous peoples.
4   TN: The Camp of the Saints.

the one we are experiencing today. The main challenge is thus for us to regain control of our own identity, affirm all that defines us and assert our firm intention to remain masters of our own destiny.

In order to meet a challenge of such magnitude, France and Europe are in need of new generations, generations that would be aware of the dangers that threaten them and their descendants, and that would be able to restore, by means of demanding intellectual work rooted in an unfailing sort of will, the very fundamentals of our history and civilisation. Such is the necessary prerequisite for the awakening of memories. Already now, a European vision is taking shape 'inside a few bold brains' inspired by both a great past and by founding myths that shall be there to channel the awakening of our peoples. We must henceforth re-establish a connection with what was and foster a new relationship to the family, our past and our physical homelands. So as to achieve this, we must adopt the notion formulated by Dominique Venner that defines 'excellence as a goal'; for it is by working on ourselves that we shall be able to forge a new kind of aristocracy based on services rendered and no longer on the derisory privileges ever so dear to the self-proclaimed pseudo-elites who, today, still have the upper hand. Indeed, it is an inner citadel that we must construct to rise to the challenges that lie ahead. Resistance against the Orwellian world that one strives to impose upon us has become a duty, regardless of the eternal pessimists who remain obsessed with lost causes and constantly repeat that the damage is already done and that our efforts shall all be in vain. For it is by converting will into action that we must respond to them, bearing in mind Hölderlin's[5] famous statement which tells us that *'where danger lies, salvation also grows.'*[6]

---

5   TN: Johann Christian Friedrich Hölderlin (1770–1843) was a German philosopher and poet.

6   TN: Because the standard translation of Hölderlin's sentence seems rather unelegant (*'Where the danger is, also grows the saving power'*), I have opted for a version that suits the English language and not the German one.

I

NATURE AS OUR FOUNDATION

'Walking through thickets or forests,
I set out to meet my own origins and eternity.'

— DOMINIQUE VENNER

(In *Dictionnaire amoureux de la chasse*[1])

---

1   TN: Hunt-Lover's Dictionary.

FROM THE REAL WORLD TO THE MARVELLOUS — RECONNECTING ARIADNE'S THREAD

BY RÉMY SOULIÉ[1]

IN THE 19th century, the geographer Élisée Reclus defined 'Man' as 'Nature becoming aware of itself', which was but a way of saying that we are not separate from the cosmos, but that the latter is, in fact, reflected in us in the specular sense, with us responding to it in the speculative sense. Later on, the anthropologist Georges Dumézil would call this representation of the presentation 'ideology', which is therefore, quite literally, a reflection, and more specifically 'all the main ideas (intellectual themes, value judgments, etc.) that remain coherent by principle and that justify, in the eyes of all those concerned, both the state of the world and their collective or individual lifestyles'.

Mythology Is Life

Originally, Indo-European man was alone in re-presenting the world in accordance with a scheme that Dumézil termed 'trifunctional', i.e. one that has three coordinated and hierarchical functions: a sovereign function, itself divided into two modes, namely the magical

---

1 TN: Born on 2 September 1968, Rémy Soulié is a French philosopher, literary critic, essayist and radio host.

and legal one; the warrior function; and the economic-productive-reproductive function. Respectively including, and without any exhaustiveness whatsoever, priests, warriors, and peasants; or, in Hindu and Guénonian terminology, the Brahmins, the Kshatriyas, and the Vaishyas; or, in the Latin, Nordic and Hindu domains, Jupiter, Mars, Quirinus; Odin-Tyr, Thor, and Freyr; Mitra-Varuna, Indra, and the Açvins; or in a historical context of Roman kingship, Romulus-Numa, Tullus Hostilius, and Ancus Marcius; and in the judgement of Paris, Hera, Athena, and Aphrodite...

Whatever it may be, the image is therefore reflected and analysed by reflection; de-composition occurs, followed by a re-composition of its elements until the elaboration of the idea is achieved, with the Greek term *eidos* designating, and most significantly at that, both the image and the idea. Successful reflection thus involves three stages: the *imaginatio vera* (meaning the image as it appears in our mind, in the form of an archetype, for instance); 'demonisation' (i.e. separation) and symbolisation (assembling).

With the reflection now accomplished, let us now call it 'thought' and understand that it is never expressed as fully as in poetry, in what Rimbaud termed 'the alchemy of the word' (which is what Heidegger also concludes), regardless of its nature or modality, whether lyrical, tragic, hymnic, political, metaphysical, epic, elegiac, pastoral, romantic, or of any other kind. In other words, the soul of a people is never understood as much as in its answers to the World Soul of *Timaeus*, in its founding or re-founding books: The *Iliad*, the *Odyssey*, Hesiod's *Theogony*, the Vedas, the Tao, the Eddas, the Bible, the Koran, the *Aeneid*, the *Grail Cycle*, *The Divine Comedy*, etc. As far as we are concerned, therefore, we have every interest in remaining attentive to lyric poets, bards, skalds and their successors.

The specifically Greek moment of our history, which is worth lingering on when one takes into account its (re-)founding character on certain levels, illustrates this very same reflexive movement most explicitly. The astonishment that accompanied the birth of philosophical poetry — or *thaumazein*, which triggers the reflexive process — was, according to Plato, simultaneously a state of wonderment. In his *Anabasis*, Xenophon reports that having climbed Madur Mountain, the Ten Thousand exclaimed: *'Thalassa! Thalassa!'*, meaning 'The sea! The sea!', which was but another way of paying tribute to a theophany, namely that of Poseidon, to this marvel of being, as it appeared to them at that time and in that very place, in all of its divine radiance. And that is what enabled Hesiod to write that 'the gods are those who have faced up [to things] in broad daylight', with Rudolf Otto stating, at a much later point, that the sacred is manifested in the *numinous* (it should indeed be noted that despite the dread aroused by the manifestations that the very term designates, one can simply replace the initial 'n' with an 'l' to land on one's feet and thus grasp a reality of which there would be much to say). Princess Europe's view encompasses a vast panorama, and in theorising, the Greeks literally contemplated (since 'to theorise' is actually 'to see a god'). All of which is but another reason to note that the artificial, academic and sterile separation of the notions of *mythos* and *logos* (of the mythical and the reasonable, to cut things short) is but a mutilation: for mytho-logy is life itself. Let us make no concessions: the real world is indeed wonderful, and it is the 'Wonder of the World' (the title of an essay by Charles Maurras[2]) that Europeans beheld for a long time before exploring the latter.

The Stone Books of Cathedrals

The slow and painful Christianisation of Europe has, of course, changed the European perception, but only up to a certain point, since Christianity, in the form of Roman Catholicism in this case, had to contend with the intrinsic paganism of European peoples. It is certainly not our intention to suggest that the idea of considering the world to have been created by a single transcendent and foreign god

---

2   TN: One of the main organisers and philosophers of Action Française, Charles Maurras was a French writer, poet, critic and politician.

that reveals himself through his prophets before sacrificing himself in payment for the sins of mankind does not, over time, noticeably alter the representations (the time in question being specifically that of the history of this 'religion of exiting religion', which is the very definition of Christianity according to Marcel Gauchet,[3] particularly because of a potential manner in which the words 'Render unto Caesar the things that are Caesar's', as stated by Jesus Christ, can be interpreted: indeed, the distinction between the temporal and the spiritual can pave the way for the latter's separation). The fact remains that, for centuries, Christianisation maintained a certain 'hinterland' (Yves Bonnefoy[4]), one that was never completely reduced to a *Hinterwelt* (Nietzsche). In addition to the fact that the particularly feudal period of the Middle Ages was organised in accordance with the tripartite ideology (the clergy, nobility, and the Third Estate) and that it continued to hold high the spiritual values of hero-warriors (i.e. those of chivalry), the *Grail Cycle* also attests to the persistence of a structurally Indo-European imagination. King Arthur was thus born of the union of Uther Pendragon and Igraine (the first function) after the former had made use of three ploys: he offered Igraine jewels and a golden cup (the third function); he fought against her lawful husband, who was his rival and vassal (second function); and he resorted to the magic of Merlin (magical sovereignty). In *The Golden Legend* by Jacobus de Voragine,[5] Saint George fights the dragon, and Saint Anthony encounters a centaur and a satyr in the desert; as for Saint Bernard, he confesses to having learned everything he knows during his stay in the forest, the oaks and beeches having been his only teachers. These are the stories that European peoples engraved into their cathedrals' stone books as they transformed the sacred stones into altars. It would be all too easy to demonstrate that this inspiration, in the most exact

---

3   TN: Marcel Gauchet is a French sociologist, historian, and philosopher.

4   TN: Born on 24 June 1923, Yves Jean Bonnefoy was a poet and art historian.

5   TN: The archbishop of Genoa, Jacobus de Voragine (1228–1298) was an Italian chronicler and author.

meaning of the word, endures to this very day, particularly through the masterpieces of two Christian writers: *The Chronicles of Narnia* by C. S. Lewis and *The Lord of the Rings* by his friend Tolkien. In the same manner, the 'lais' written by Marie de France; the tales penned by the Grimm brothers, Perrault and Andersen; popular traditions; and folklore have pieced together and enriched this profound memory. From this point of view, is not the historian Jacques Le Goff right to regard the period extending from late antiquity to the Industrial Revolution as a long mediaeval one?

The Naked Goddess

Three previous revolutions, namely the Lutheran, Galileo-Cartesian and Kantian ones (which occurred respectively in the 16th, 17th and 18th centuries), had nonetheless contributed to confusing minds by combining the discourse of subjectivity with that of scientific objectivity. The subject and the object, matter and spirit, earth and heaven, mythos and logos were thus dissociated in the minds of men, when, in actual fact, they obviously remain united. No dryad seems to inhabit the *res extensa* any longer — the ponderable, measurable, and calculable 'extended thing' that can be chopped up into pieces, which, when burning, have the potential to release energy that will set the machine in motion. No one sees fairies anymore, except for the Scottish reverend Robert Kirk, who set off after them and is said to have succumbed to an 'elf-shot', an arrow that does not kill you but takes your soul away to Fairyland (indeed, the reverend is alleged to have been exceedingly curious and talkative). Enchantments and grace have vanished due to their lack of efficacy when compared to the 'efficiency' of the masters and rulers of nature. Europeans now spend less time watching the stars, the beautiful mistresses of order and destiny, than they invest in the technological organisation of their Faustian conquest... without involving love or, to use Empedocles'[6] words,

---

6   TN: A native of the Greek Sicilian city of Akragas, Empedocles was a philosopher.

'sympathy' in the process. They have lifted the veil of Isis-Physis, of Artemis *multimammia*, of Heraclitus'[7] 'Nature [that] loves to hide', and have judged the goddess to be naked; despite the warnings of both Novalis[8] and Hölderlin, they thus scrutinised her in anticipation of the total commitment of all beings. In this sense, Heidegger[9] interprets the history of Western metaphysics as being that of the oblivion of Being; which is also why he assesses that 'only a god can save us now' from nihilism (whose secularisation is but a mediocre avatar) — although he does also teach us, along with Hölderlin once again, that 'where danger lies, salvation also grows'. And that is precisely why, in this age that obviously embodies the final phase of the cycle, a new dawn is inevitably breaking.

Merlin's Light

First of all, we do know how to read the correct alphabet — that of the language of mythology. We must therefore read our own history using its own terms, simply because it is ours; as if it were, in this particular case, the expression of a conflict between the poet Orpheus and the Titan Prometheus, a conflict which, along with other ones, is in line with our own destiny, we who know that Polemos[10] is indeed the father of all things. As part of the phase that we are currently going through, the Titans have thus resurfaced, which means that we have to perceive and understand our world not so much in accordance with the Weberian[11] logic of disenchantment as in harmony with the

---

7   TN: Born in the city of Ephesus, Heraclitus was a Greek pre-Socratic philosopher.

8   TN: Known by his pen name Novalis, Georg Philipp Freiherr von Hardenberg (1772–1801) was a German aristocrat, writer, poet, philosopher and mystic.

9   TN: Martin Heidegger (1889–1976) is one of Germany's most famous philosophers.

10   TN: The divine personification of war.

11   TN: Based on the socio-economic theories formulated by Max Weber.

wise Artaudian[12] madness of enchantment: 'The world — that of our current earth, *and especially that of the current European earth* [as emphasised by us] — is governed by a series of coordinated and calculated enchantments...'

Indeed, 'there is a certain matter of global possession', writes admirably *le Mômo*,[13] who could be described, just like Nerval[14] according to Baudelaire,[15] as having always been lucid. And because we do know how to read the correct alphabet, we must perceive and understand that the dark side of Merlin (the devil's son) has temporarily prevailed over the bright one (the son of the virgin). It is only under such conditions that the darkness will begin to dissipate and we can hope to behold the first glimmers of a new beginning.

Furthermore, we have never actually left — and for good reason, as it is an impossible feat — the *Unus mundus* of Gerhard Dorn and Jung, the 'one world' that comprises an infinite number of levels (from the crudest to the most subtle) and in which all illusory dualities are resorbed, including those of transcendence and immanence. The thread of Ariadne that guides us along our 'path to the inside', as worded by Novalis, is secret and esoteric, unfolding inconspicuously through time and slipping into religious dogmas; nihilistic devastation is powerless against it, since it has already integrated it by recognising it as its own shadow. It has never snapped and never will. It does not relate to an act of faith, but to knowledge, to a 'shared birth' that is by no means foreign to Claudelian[16] gnosis. The golden chain of those who have spun it is very long indeed: Pythagoras and the Presocratics, Plato, Plotinus, Proclus, Porphyry, Jamblichus, Pseudo-Dionysius the

---

12   TN: Relating to Antoine Marie Joseph Paul Artaud (1896–1948), who was active as a a poet, essayist, actor, dramatist, theatre director and writer.

13   TN: *Artaud le Mômo* is Artaud's most acclaimed poetic work.

14   TN: Born Gérard Labrunie, Nerval was a prominent figure of French romanticism.

15   TN: Charles Baudelaire is arguably the most famous French poet of all time.

16   TN: Relating to Paul Claudel, a French diplomat, dramatist and poet.

Areopagite, John Scotus Eriugena, Hildegard of Bingen, Meister Eckart, Angelus Silesius, Nicholas of Cusa, Giovanni Pico della Mirandola, Marsilio Ficino, Paracelsus, Giordano Bruno, Jakob Boehme, Emanuel Swedenborg, Franz von Baader, Guénon, Evola, Carl Gustav Jung, Mircea Eliade, Henry Corbin, and others. On the scientific front, energy lies at the very heart of matter and the observer interacts with what he observes, with quantum physicist Wolfgang Pauli calling for the establishment of 'background physics', to which one would have to be truly deaf to fail to perceive it as a 'hinterland'.

Beyond all dualism, and beyond Aristotelian and scholastic logic and the various frigid (and therefore vicious) mechanisms that it has engendered, this secret Europe — one of whose physical and spiritual homes can be found in Stefan George's secret Germany — remains poetically and therefore genuinely inhabitable. Whosoever lives there will have their eyes opened, as the correspondences between microcosm and macrocosm burst forth, synchronicities abound and characteristics unfurl in as many manifestations of immanent transcendence. Through experience, nature reverts to being the wonderland it has never ceased to be, namely that of the *Mysterium conjunctionis*.

According to Hölderlin, the closest is also the most difficult to attain, as it requires the organic dynamics of a 'patriotic reversal'. Such is the destination, living relationship and destiny reserved for us Hesperians — to reconnect with the all, with the safe, in the sacred night of modernity.

Bibliographical References

Yves Bonnefoy, *L'Arrière-pays*,[17] Gallimard, collection Poésie/Gallimard, 2005.
Pierre Hadot, *Le Voile d'Isis*,[18] Gallimard, collection Folio, 2008.
Carl Gustav Jung, *Mysterium conjunctionis*, Volume I and II, Albin Michel, 1980, 1982.

17　TN: The Hinterland.
18　TN: The Veil of Isis.

Robert Kirk, *The Secret Commonwealth of Elves, Fauns & Fairies: A Study in Folklore & Psychical Research*, Elf-Shot, 2016.

Plato, *Timaeus-Critias*, translated from Ancient Greek by L. Brisson and M. Patillon, Flammarion, collection GF, 2017.

FOR AN ECOLOGY OF PEOPLES: NATURE AS THE FOUNDATION OF IDENTITY

BY HENRI LEVAVASSEUR[1]

T RUMPET CALLS for the 'rescue of nature' are now resounding from all sides: they are, however, not devoid of political afterthoughts and inconsistencies. Indeed, can one truly denounce the ravages caused by mass production and the consumer society without renouncing the myth of indefinite progress and development? Or deplore the environmental effects of globalisation while simultaneously advocating the implementation of a global governance system? Or highlight the disastrous consequences of liberal economic deregulation while extolling the benefits of a libertarian vision of both man and society? For there is no credible ecology in the absence of a realistic anthropology. In truth, it is not a question of 'saving the planet': being more ancient than the appearance of man on its surface, it could survive perfectly well without him in future. The main issue is to maintain the existential conditions of our species, which necessarily involves a fundamental reflection on the essence of human nature, for it is this very essence that constitutes the foundation upon which we we can erect a code of ethics, that is to say a specific way of remaining in this

---

1   TN: Henri Levavasseur is a French author specialising in history.

world and taking care of it, all in accordance with the *mos maiorum*,
i.e. the custom established by our ancestors.

A Cultural Being by Nature

Defined as the science that studies the behaviour of species, ethology
teaches us that, unlike animals, man is not a 'specialised being', one that
possesses innate qualities that enable him to adapt spontaneously to a
specific environment. Indeed, man is born without claws, without fur,
and with undeveloped instincts. In compensation for this, his perspective turns out to be less limited than that of animals, whose existence is
closely connected with their specific biotope. As remarked by biologist
Konrad Lorenz, man is a 'specialist of non-speciality', possessing, on
the other hand, an obvious 'aptitude for youthfulness': whatever nature
failed to endow him with at birth man acquires through learning and
the action of his own hands, which constitutes what the Greeks termed
'technique'. The myth of Epimetheus perfectly illustrates this particu-
larity, which is both a deficiency and a strength: tasked by Zeus with
allocating qualities and attributes to animals, the Titan Epimetheus
carried out this task without leaving anything useful for men, who
thus remained vulnerable until Prometheus stole the gods' divine fire
for them.

The opinion expressed by the philosopher and anthropologist
Arnold Gehlen is completely in line with this ancient conception
when characterising man as an 'incomplete being', one that is left
unfinished at birth, which defines him as a being that is 'open to the
world': although ignorant while in their cradle, children gradually
learn to dominate their environment and to communicate with their
peers thanks to what they are taught by those closest to them. Man is,
therefore, a 'cultural being by nature' — and consequently a social one.
The development of our intelligence is closely linked to the learning of
a language, a language that acts as both heir and bearer of a culture that
underpins our vision of the world and structures our very thinking.
There is therefore no natural state whose existence precedes that of

society, as believed by Hobbes,[2] much less some abstract individuals with pre-existing universal rights that predate the 'social contract', as claimed by some thinkers of the Enlightenment.

The emergence of a culture is always intimately linked to a territory, which implies a notion of borders and boundaries: for every culture is the product of the history of a specific people, of a particular human group within a delimited geographical space. Borders and boundaries should, however, not be perceived as shackles that restrain us, but as conditions for the existence of human cultures in all their diversity. During his beautiful reflection on the high relief of the Acropolis representing the goddess Athena leaning over a border-stone, Heidegger emphasised that a boundary is certainly 'not only outline and frame, […] the place where something stops. Boundary means that through which something is gathered into its ownmost aspect, in order to appear thereby in all its fullness'.

Existing Through What Sets Us Apart

No culture can evolve in the absence of social order and institutions. What follows from this is that, as stated by Aristotle, 'the city exists by nature', and 'man is by nature a political animal'. A stateless person, adds Aristotle, incurs the reproaches expressed by Homer and targeting every 'tribeless, homeless, lawless' man. For man does not exist separately from others, in the manner of a Cartesian subject, before establishing a connection with the world: open to the world from the very outset, he is shaped by his inheritance of a specific culture, which, in turn, renders him capable of founding his own inner world. Such is the full meaning of Joseph de Maistre's famous statement:

> There is no such thing as man in this world. I have encountered Frenchmen, Italians, and Russians; thanks to Montesquieu, I now even know that one

---

2   TN: Known for his elaborate formulation of what is termed 'social contract theory', Thomas Hobbes (1588–1679) was an English philosopher.

can be Persian; as for man himself, I declare that I have never met him in
my entire life; if indeed he does exist, I am definitely not aware of it.

Similarly, Dominique Venner writes that 'men exist in diversity only
through what distinguishes them, namely their clans, peoples, nations,
cultures, and civilisations, and not through what they have in common
on the surface of things. The only universal thing is their animality'.
Just as no tree can live without roots, the universal only exists as a
polyphonic extension of specific identities.

Although based on the precepts of ancient wisdom as substanti-
ated by modern European scientific breakthroughs, this realistic conception of human nature is now fiercely contested by the proponents
of a new perception of man and society, one that is both profoundly
subversive and totalitarian.

In the name of the fight against all forms of discrimination, 'clean
slate' supporters are determined to deconstruct the categories of classical anthropology. They intend to impose once and for all, first through
media and social pressure and then by means of legal and statal constraints, the model of 'fluid' identities that are meant to replace 'natural'
families and peoples, entities that are deemed oppressive or outdated.
From this perspective, the sovereign individual must be able to choose
his own identity in complete autonomy, with social order having no
other function than to guarantee the exercise of such free will. This
doxa is being applied to the domain of gender identity, postulating the
existence of 'gender' categories that have become entirely independent
of biological facts. It is also spreading through the field that appertains
to the identity of peoples and nations, both of which are thus reduced
to an arbitrary and purely contractual structure in which one's feeling
of belonging to the same ethno-cultural community is no longer of
any relevance.

This death-dealing ideology, however, comes up against the walls
of reality, both on the level of individuals and that of peoples: the progress made over the past few decades in terms of genetic research now

makes it possible for us to identify the distant origins of a population using DNA extracted from human remains that, at times, are very old indeed. The results of these analyses indicate that most peoples stem from the interbreeding of different human groups, all, however, in accordance with methods and ratios that bestow upon each one of them a specific identity, making it impossible to reduce their history to a mere phenomenon of incessant interbreeding. With regard to Europe, paleo-geneticists have highlighted the presence of three ancestral populations: the oldest is that of indigenous hunter-gatherers, who, from the seventh millennium B.C. onwards, first mingled with farmers of Anatolian origin, and then, beginning in the fourth millennium, with several waves of conquerors arriving from the southern steppes of present-day Russia. And it was probably the latter who imposed, wherever they settled, the language defined since the end of the 19th century as the Indo-European one, the original matrix of all the languages still spoken on our continent, with the exception of the Basque and Finno-Ugric languages. No newer contribution has, to this very day, come to modify on such a large scale the genetic heritage and linguistic identity of almost all European peoples. The main ethno-cultural groups of ancient Europe mostly stem from this common crucible: indeed, regardless of whether one is focusing on ancient Greece and Rome, Germanic peoples, Celts, Balts or Slavs, all are, to varying degrees, bearers of the Indo-European heritage, in combination with more ancient substratums.

Identity as One's Heritage

Paleo-genetic facts thus converge to a large extent with those of linguistics, archeology and history. It should be noted that the modern European peoples whose language does not belong to the Indo-European family (the Basques, Hungarians, Finns, and Estonians) have nonetheless been part of the civilisational framework of Christian Europe for centuries, a framework inherited to a large extent from the Roman imperial world. In the absence of political unity, therefore,

Europe's geographical space clearly coincides with the existence of a group of peoples closely related in terms of origin, culture and customs.

This digression along the path of Europe's most ancient past takes us directly to the very heart of our current topic. In contrast with the quixotic notion of individuals endowed with a 'self-shaping' capacity and having an absolute right to free themselves from biological, hereditary and community-related conditioning, one had better remember that man is, first and foremost, a 'social and political animal', one whose profound nature is determined by the twofold heritage passed down by those who preceded it: on the one hand, the bequeathment of a language and a culture, and on the other , that of a genetic heritage. On a collective scale, this dual heritage embodies the identity of a people, alongside the customs and worldview connected with it.

This identity is not frozen in time, in the sense understood by those who denounce the misguided ways of so-called 'essentialism'. Dominique Venner responded masterfully to this objection when he defined tradition as 'a whisper of ancient and future times', as 'that which perseveres and crosses time itself'. For it is not limited to the past, but on the contrary represents 'that which does not pass. It comes to us from the most distant times, yet is still relevant. It is our inner compass'. As for Heidegger, he conjures up a similar vision in relation to the dawn of Greece's golden age: 'The beginning has invaded our future. There it awaits us, a distant command bidding us catch up with its greatness'.

For a Peoples' Ecology

Identity is a potential that we are to realise in harmony with modalities that remain specific to the contingencies of the moment, so as to attune ourselves to our destiny. Indeed, the peoples of Europe are the bearers of a specific ethnic and cultural heritage and have every right to want to transmit this heritage across the geographical space that they have shaped for themselves in accordance with their own capabilities and within the civilisational framework that is theirs, particularly through the establishment of the traditional family, which acts as the guardian of our memory and heredity. And it is this fundamental right that we demand for our peoples, a right that Pope Francis readily acknowledges when it comes to Amazonian tribes but denies to Europeans, who are being told to open their doors without any resistance whatsoever.

Properly understood, ecology consists not only in protecting animal species, but also in preserving the diversity of peoples 'as they have been shaped by thousands of years of long patience', to use Jean Mabire's[3] beautiful phrase. For it is by restoring his keen awareness of his own specificity that European man will be able to start cultivating a particular form of excellence in conformity with his very nature, by rejecting such 'metaphysics of the unlimited', whose excessiveness represents the ultimate driving force of modernity.

In contrast with the desire to 'always have more', a man with strong roots espouses the logic of 'always doing better'. Faithful to an ethical principle that remains in tune with his own tradition, he thus ceases to regard the earth as an inexhaustible source of benefits whose un-bridled exploitation helps to maintain the illusion of a trajectory of infinite growth, development and progress. Let us therefore adopt Friedrich Hölderlin's words according to which 'man lives as a poet', so that the world may once again gradually become, from our perspective, what Martin Heidegger termed 'the fourfold': 'earth, sky, mortals and divinities'. For it is on this very basis that it becomes possible for us to formulate the 'right' sort of ecology, one that can provide us with answers equal to the challenges that lie ahead.

Bibliographical References

Arnold Gehlen, *Essais d'anthropologie philosophique*,[4] Maison des Sciences de l'Homme, collection Bibliothèque allemande, 2010.

---

3   TN: Born on 8 February 1927, Jean Mabire was a French essayist and journalist.
4   TN: Essays on Political Anthropology.

Arnold Gehlen, *Der Mensch: Seine Natur und seine Stellung in der Welt*[5] — translated from German by C. Sommer, Gallimard. Published in 2021.

Martin Heidegger, *Vorträge und Aufsätze*,[6] Günther Neske, 1954. Translated from German by A. Préau. Preface by J. Beaufret. Gallimard, collection Tel, 1980.

Konrad Lorenz, *Über tierisches und menschliches Verhalten*,[7] translated from German by C. et P. Fredet, Seuil, 1970.

Nouvelle École — *Paléogénétique des Indo-Européens*,[8] issue number 68, 2019.

---

5   TN : Man, His Nature and Place in the World.

6   TN: Lectures and Essays.

7   TN: Studies in Human and Animal Behaviour.

8   TN: Indo-European Paleogenetics.

NATURE AND TERRITORY — BECOMING THE ARCHITECTS OF OUR OWN LANDSCAPE ONCE AGAIN

BY JEAN-PHILIPPE ANTONI[1]

E COLOGY AND environmental sciences have established a very clear link between the life of ecosystems and the delimitation of territories. Outside its own territory, meaning its biotope, an animal cannot subsist nor a plant survive: indeed, there are no polar bears in the savannah nor palm trees on ice floes. Beyond the climatic conditions and resources that it brings, a territory also constitutes a fundamental action medium that conditions the different types of behaviour necessary to ensure the survival and reproduction of a given species. For this purpose, the vast majority of animals are endowed with encoded responses: an animal knows instinctively what it can or should eat, how to defend itself and how to hunt. It generally displays cautious behaviour when exiting its own territory. Within the latter, however, it quickly becomes aggressive to avoid intrusions. In the plant world, plants sense the importance of light and grow in a manner allowing

---

1   TN: Jean-Philippe Antoni is a French geographer.

them to benefit from it, sometimes at the expense of other plants that they eliminate from their immediate vicinity.

Territory, the Foundation of Identity

So what about man? Man is also an element of living ecosystems and subject to specific existential conditions. In terms of reacting to the constraints of the natural environment, however, he suffers from a lack of innate behaviour and has no ready-made answer to the information he receives from nature, a fact that led Nietzsche to describe him as 'the not yet fixed animal', one whose essence is not conclusively established from the very outset. Moreover, compared to the members of the animal world, man is physiologically poorly equipped: he is very weak when it comes to both his natural defence capacities (since he has no shell, fur, etc.) and attacking abilities (claws, jaw, etc.), and seems more or less 'naked' in the face of aggression and exposure to the environment. Despite these 'defects', man does have, on the other hand, a considerable advantage: innovation. Indeed, he possesses certain skills that allow him to resolve the problems posed by adaptation. Furthermore, as summarised by Arnold Gehlen, man does not actually adapt to the natural environment — instead, he adapts the latter to himself. Rather than saying that he is incapable of adaptation, we could also emphasise his human specificity by stressing the fact that he is made to have nature adapt to him. So as to ensure his own survival and reproduction, he is, in fact, even *forced* to do so.

Consequently, man has no specific natural environment, i.e. no biotope of his own: each is hostile at the beginning (though some much more than others), yet all can be adapted and be made liveable. Indeed, it is in man's very nature to create his own territory and develop his own landscapes, an aspect that is inextricably linked to the development of his own culture. And in order for him to do this, the natural characteristics (or physiological matrix) shared by the entire homo sapiens species come across as much less decisive than the neotenic development of an autonomous culture (or social matrix).

What follows from this is that from a biological nature that is probably identical, several variants have surfaced within human societies.

The relationship between territory and society is therefore an ambivalent one: people organise themselves in a society in order to forge their own territory, and it is during this very shaping process that society-fashioning behaviour, knowledge, techniques and exchanges emerge. One's territory must therefore be considered a 'social product': society perpetuates itself through the construction of its living space. In the eyes of geographer Hildebert Isnard, 'society takes form when rooted in its own culture and space; as soon as it is deprived of this space, it disintegrates. Should it be forced to adapt to an environment that is imposed upon it, it loses a part of its original organic identity'. Understood in such a context, a territory is an intrinsic part of society, not only because it enables the latter's biological survival, but also because it organises its entire existence.

This essential connection with one's territory does, however, remain 'flexible', which partly explains the reason behind human ubiquity: man lives virtually everywhere (across all six continents), regardless of any ecological conditions that limit animal or plant establishment. This flexibility presupposes two possible conditions: man can either adapt his way of life to the environment, which requires his acceptance of potentially limited comfort, or transform this medium so as to maximise his own comfort, which implies the presence of complex environmental features and necessitates an in-depth sort of development. And this development can only be achieved through the exploitation of available ecological resources, i.e. through the existence of other (animal and plant) species present in the same place.

The second option is obviously the more common one. The ecumene has now been completely developed by man to enable him to survive and live in an environment for which he lacks the natural and appropriate biology and behaviour. With the spread of man and his activities across the entire planet, the natural environment has thus automatically retreated in three successive historical stages. *First* came man's *adaptation* to nature, with a passive use of resources, the invention of tools, gathering and hunting during the more or less nomadic pastoral stage of the Paleolithic. The *next phase* was that of the *enslavement* of nature through agriculture and the sedentarisation of rural societies, lasting from the Neolithic to the 17th century approximately. As for the *third* phase, it involved the *creation* (from scratch) of a territory exclusively dedicated to the fulfilment of human needs without the restrictions of natural ecosystems — industry, technological development, and the urbanisation of the 17th and 18th centuries, all of which led to unprecedented changes in terms of planetary balance.

For the Right Kind of Ecology

The forging of a territory implies a progressive mastery of nature, one which, in turn, presupposes a 'useful artificialisation' of a certain part of the wild world. Indeed, the only species allowed to stand alongside humans are all domesticated, meaning that they can be increased, transported and altered. Selected for productivity reasons, Angus bulls, Yorkshire pigs and Holstein cows exemplify, in this regard, the most remarkable of achievements. The finest example, however, is certainly that of dogs, of which man has produced, by means of repeated crossbreeding, a multitude of breeds that cater to his needs and whims: they are thus useful in terms of shepherding (for all kinds of shepherds and herdsmen) and cynegetics (hunting dogs themselves have their own specialisation: hounds, pointers, retriever dogs, search or tracking dogs, etc.). They can also have a martial function (including army dogs, police dogs and watchdogs, which often come from a long line of shepherd dogs) or play a social role (pet dogs, guide dogs, etc.).

In the plant world, corn is another example of useful artificialisation: resulting from a hybridisation of teosinte, it is now so far removed from its natural strain that it can no longer survive outside human activity. Equally common, grapevines are also a prime example: pruning, removing side-shoots, pinching back shoot tips, trimming, leaf removal, and tendril removal are all processing techniques that increase the sugar concentration and that have profoundly altered the appearance of a plant that originally belonged to the creeper family. On the other hand, this artificialisation of nature is responsible for a culture-transforming change to our ways of life: provocatively, we could say that it was man who created the grapevine, and that drunkenness created the gods 'connected with it' (Dionysus for the Greeks and Bacchus for the Romans) prior to the latter's knowledge of man…

From man's perspective, the alteration of ecological balances thus constitutes a 'normal' action: indeed, he uses it for his own sustenance while simultaneously striving to fight against the disorder that he himself thus causes and that jeopardises the very subsistence that he hopes to derive from it. At a time when such transformations are made possible through genetic intervention (GMOs), one can genuinely wonder what is still natural about the thing we continue to call 'nature'. This situation, however, which is sometimes disastrous in terms of maintaining both the current climatic conditions and biodiversity, brings to mind an absolutely inescapable fact: modifying ecosystems — sometimes significantly — in order to establish a liveable territory and protect oneself from a hostile environment by mastering it is simply mandatory. This reality must be seen as the primary axiom of what is truly the right kind of ecology.

Reconstructing Our Landscapes

Every society creates its own landscape according to its own culture, social prism and know-how, deriving from it a territory that is also specific. The ecumene should therefore not be understood as a universal and neutral space that is said to evenly cover the entire planet; on the contrary, it is highly differentiated and corresponds to a juxtaposition of more or less autonomous cultural areas, some of which are connected to each other and some separated by natural barriers or borders. The structure of societies, their way of life and their connection with the world are clearly expressed through these geographies, which give specific shape to the way in which the former have chosen to inscribe (graphy) their presence on the terrestrial plane (geo). To those who know how to interpret it, this identity is clearly legible on a map.

Ever since mankind entered the Anthropocene, however (with the industrialisation of various techniques intended to transform nature, in addition to the globalised flow of information, people and goods), these considerations have only been partly valid. Widespread urbanisation has acted as a formidable machine to standardise territories and erase connections with whatever nature is left there. Urban climate is an excellent example of this. Having long been based on observation (that of clouds, wind characteristics and the flight of birds), weather forecasting now uses tools instead (thermometers, anemometers, balloons, radars, and satellites). This constitutes a first type of ancestral and direct knowledge that has been lost to an artificial and indirect sort of mediation which correlates to technical and scientific progress. To Jacques Ellul,[2] this technological-scientific mediation is now complete, forming a continuous and extensive screen separating man from nature: such is the 'technical domain', which has replaced ecosystems by becoming the prime medium of a transposable urban culture that remains disconnected from the realities of the world; which is why it has become useful to explain to school children that no breaded fish is born rectangular and that minced turkey does not grow under cellophane in trees…

Beyond Pierre Le Vigan's[3] criticism of the 'obesity' of megacities, however, land-use planning is a legacy that remains inscribed into the landscapes and which Europe abounds in particularly. Indeed, ever since Antiquity or the Middle Ages, its villages have been erected around the symbol of crossroads and the Church, its market places

---

2   TN: Jacques Ellul (1912–1994) was a rather complex intellectual, working as a philosopher, sociologist, (lay) theologian and professor. He is also known to have been a Christian anarchist.

3   TN: Pierre Le Vigan is a French essayist, journalist and philosopher with close ties to the French New Right.

remaining accessible both on foot and on horseback. The location of its villages and cities have enabled the complementarity of urban and rural areas, their symbolism characterised by remarkable architecture and vernacular city planning. To preserve this culture and identity is to become aware of the social reality shaped by territories. Indeed, our age-old Europe has been the architect of its own landscape equilibrium — to erase or renounce the latter in favour of uniform living arrangements would constitute an irreparable amputation of the territorial medium that simultaneously contains all the unity and diversity of the European identity.

Bibliographical References

Arnold Gehlen, *Essais d'anthropologie philosophique*, Maison des Sciences de l'Homme, collection Bibliothèque allemande, 2010.

Hildebert Isnard, *Problématique de la géographie*,[4] Presses universitaires de France, 1981.

Isidore Geoffroy Saint-Hilaire, *Domestication et naturalisation des animaux utiles*,[5] Dusacq, 1854.

Jacques Ellul, *Le Système technicien*,[6] Le Cherche midi, 1977.

Pierre Le Vigan, *Métamorphoses de la ville*,[7] La Barque d'or, 2020.

---

4   TN: The Problematic of Geography.

5   TN: The Domestication and Naturalisation of Useful Animals.

6   TN: The Technical System.

7   TN: Urban Metamorphoses.

MAN AND HIS NATURE — SHAPING THE DESTINY OF THE CITY-STATE

BY JEAN-FRANÇOIS GAUTIER[1]

I N THE 21st century, adopting nature as a foundation for one's reflections and actions is not synonymous with opting for a rural life by a river, but with choosing a certain ethical and political way of life. Admittedly, the general topic of the very naturalness of man has, over the centuries, given rise to endless arguments — which is due to the simple fact that each of the two related terms, namely 'nature' and 'mankind', has its own ambiguities, which, in themselves, reflect a wide range of beliefs and ideologies. Among our contemporaries, the idea of nature refers rather to the scientific domain, and that of humanity rather to law, i.e. to two different notions which, if not antagonistic, are at least kept distinct by their very methods, interests and issues.

A Naturally Political Man

It would be useful here to shift one's viewpoint and adopt Aristotle's for a moment, if only to unravel those lines of thought that modern discussions on nature have now terribly muddled. In his *Politics* (1253a9),

---

1   TN: A man of many skills, Jean-François Gautier is a French journalist, author, editor, etiopath, musicologist and philosopher.

Aristotle thus states that 'the city is one of those things that are by nature' and that 'a human being is by nature an animal meant for a city'. He wrote these words, of course, at a time when his former pupil Alexander of Macedon was in his process of building an empire, i.e. a set of power-based interrelations whose regulating principles would reach far beyond those of the ancient city that acted as an Aristotelian model.

Even in a modern context, however, Aristotle's reflections are a source of useful observations that contrast with contractualist theories. Very common in political ideologies since the days of Rousseau[2] and Hobbes, the latter have led everyone to forget that the city to which they belong surpasses them — in other words, that, prior to there being any contract, everyone is born 'by nature' into a whole that precedes them, thus being but a part among other parts that were active long before they ever came to be.

Properly understood, Aristotle's thought leads us further still. Indeed, when he states that a human being is, by nature, a political being, i.e. a city-dwelling one, he could simply be making an observation on herd behaviour: for all animals tend to congregate and live in groups, even bees, which, owing to their very nature, also gather in an organised way. In addition, many animals have, just like humans, a vocal organ allowing them to communicate. And yet men are the only ones, according to Aristotle, to be endowed with 'the logos' and have an actual language. Modern naturalists would of course say that among other animals, dolphins or bonobos also have a language. In advance, however, Aristotle adds a decisive point: when congregating, only humans make use of a language which, in addition to voicing one's joy and pain, makes it possible to define what a person is experiencing as advantageous or harmful, just or unjust, expressing many

---

2   TN: Jean-Jacques Rousseau was a Genevan author, composer and philosopher whose writings and views contributed greatly to the Enlightenment period, the French Revolution and modern thought.

other feelings and states which, when combined, contribute to delineating 'the household and the City', both of which obviously precede individuals.

It is clear that what Aristotle is referring to here using the term 'nature' encompasses, from our contemporary perspective, two very different domains. That the city should be 'one of those things that are by nature' is a source of shock to modern people: to them, there is always a collective reality that precedes the person that has just been born, the one who has just arrived, but it is a question of chronology, not one of 'nature'. Conversely, human gatherings, the human voice, and the expression of feelings that serve the common good and the city-state are all alleged to belong to the domain of biology or, from a more general perspective, to that of the life sciences that study nature as such. From an ancient point of view, however, this distinction is nowhere to be seen: both the anteriority of the city and the physiological characteristics of living beings are part of the general category of 'what does not depend on us', thus relating to a 'necessity' (*ananke*), which is a primary feature of *physis* or nature. It is therefore definitely 'by nature' that a Hellenic man is born in a city (a city in the general sense) and by accident in a certain empirical city, whether Athens or Sparta, which, in fact, only exist through the slow application or repeated use of natural physical qualities (voice, feelings) that citizens naturally resort to so as to contribute to one common good or another, a common good that is not universal but specific to each particular city. In every one of them, language differs as much as the assessment of what is just and unjust; of how close humans are to animals, plants or gods; and so on. In other words, citizens are, by nature, beings of culture, i.e. beings of difference that produce a variety of political formations.

The Nature of the City

This change of point of view can now turn out to be heuristic. At this time of identification crises, when democracy supporters no longer know what to describe as liberal, illiberal, decaying, decayed or dictatorial, a good way to redefine images and arguments is to contemplate the extent to which, among Europeans, the first *natural* fact is that of the city—which is not the case of the more directly tribal, African, Amerindian or Oceanian representations. Unsurprisingly, modern cities, and especially mega-cities and megalopolises, no longer correspond in any way to the direct understanding that ancient observers must have had of their own cities. This, however, is precisely one of the functions of the analysis of political representations, namely to determine whether the size of cities and the modern obsolescence of the expression of feelings relating to both usefulness and harmfulness—which have nowadays been deprived of all institutional channels, as seen in the case of the yellow vests—are not the primary causes behind the devaluation of political organisations that burdens our contemporary states.

With regard to civic naturality, Aristotle remarks (*Politics*, 1253a27) that 'one who is no part of a city, either from lacking the power to be in an association or from needing nothing on account of self-sufficiency, is for that reason either a beast or a god. So the impulse toward this sort of association [a city] is in all people by nature'. From this point of view, the fact of adopting nature as the foundation of our political thought, and of our thoughts in general, enables us to easily appraise all the modern representations of nature (which are very limited compared to those of old), i.e. the entire physico-chemical and biological environment that is part of the same nature as us humans.

Against Nature?

The ideologies that revolve around the notion of the 'individual-contractor' will obviously consider environmental protection as an obvious expression of the common interest of all parties involved in the contract. Hence an infinite conceptual extension of this status of contracting party, of the individual citizen, now applicable to all the inhabitants of the planet as a result of their having interconnected interests. This numerical representation, however, is not devoid of theoretical and practical difficulties: indeed, it may be (or actually is) in the common interest of a certain number of individuals or institutions, whether financially or otherwise, not to contribute to the preservation of their physico-chemical or biological environment. This conflict of interests thus becomes a major issue.

Such a conflict, furthermore, is not merely a matter of opposing sides, since it is also present within the sides themselves, as seen, for example, when numerous individuals or groups declare themselves in favour of limiting the consumption of fossil fuels without actually reducing their own heating or electricity consumption nor restricting their car journeys in any way. This is just as true in the case of those ethnic groups that practice slash-and-burn agriculture and set light to thousands of hectares of savannas or forests without being able to control the fire's expansion. The conflict of interests is blatant here, even if it can sometimes come across as unintentional, that is to say, innocent.

To avoid having one's thoughts wander in infinitely numerous directions, which, for the most part, are a-political and characteristic of the prominence of the individual citizen, it would be useful, at least from the perspective of the Europeans that inherit such understanding, to center one's representations on the following essential reality: the first fact of nature — in relation to the individuals that comprise it — is the city; and from this perspective, it is obviously impossible to balance the relations that connect the latter with the rest of *physis* (nature) if one fails to implement and express the feelings (*aisthesis*) that naturally contribute to the *common good*, which is collective and differs from the notion of *common interests*, which, for their part, remain individual despite being shared.

Shaping Our Destiny

What comes in at this stage in the thoughts of anyone who adopts nature as the very foundation of their own representations is their awareness of a basic fact: the respective histories of ancient cities reveal that their achievements were not homogeneous (Athens, for instance, differed from Sparta) nor consistently successful (Greece itself was the setting for many wars between different cities, before being invaded by Roman troops) — which obviously means that the very nature that *establishes* the city as a human cornerstone is not, in itself, a mechanism involved in the specifics that characterise the future development of empirical cities. The conceptual space that thus separates origin from becoming and development is what Hellenic mentalities termed *Heimarmene* or *Moira* and the Latins *fatum* or *fortuna*, meaning destiny (Cicero, *De divinatione*, I, 55: 'Now by Fate I mean the same that the Greeks call "heimarmene".'

In this difference between what naturally gives rise to the city and what characterises the destiny-related becoming or development of empirical cities, a number of later theologies would, for fear of tainting the divine with the misguided and erring ways of man, choose to detect the freedom of action given to the children of God. In his *Candide*, Voltaire would point out that the people of Lisbon had had no freedom with regard to the earthquake that devastated Lisbon in November 1755. Such is the difference between shaped destiny and endured destiny. And it is for this very reason that, in order to anticipate, counter or cope with the vagaries imposed upon every city's future by nature itself, excellence in action must be a goal, and beauty a horizon of achievements. For these regulators are valid in and of themselves — indeed, they do not transform political communities into municipal collectivities and, above all, refrain from shattering all hope when current events are darkened by the blackest of clouds, by events that go against people's most fervently shared wishes.

It is clear that in its representation of the city, modern thought would do well to re-learn how to connect the necessary, which characterises the civic nature of Europeans, with the uncertainty of a history to be shaped, a history that is always unexpected and unpredictable. In short, although the fact of striving to 'shape a history', namely that of the city, arises from natural necessities, this history is such that daily unpredictable branchings are encountered along the path. Hence the ambiguity, equivocation and, by the same token, wealth of this type of commitment, one that is specific to European traditions: choosing nature as the representative foundation of one's individual or civic life constitutes a decisive manner of combining the (political) necessity of collective action with the (ethical) contingent of its practical implementation, all of which are things that contemporary individualism has, for decades, been striving to circumvent.

With individualism defined by modern philosophies and ideologies as one of the manifestations of the uncoupling of two conflicting representations, namely that of nature and that of the city, it is reasonable to assume that their re-arranging will make it possible for us to redefine the political sphere and overcome, by means of an adventurous choice of path, the representative and organisational crises that characterise contemporary democracies.

Bibliographical References

Aristotle, *Physics*, translated from Ancient Greek by P. Pellegrin, Flammarion, collection GF, 1999.

Lucien Jerphagnon, *Histoire de la pensée, Tome 1*,[3] Antiquité et Moyen Âge, Tallandier, 1989.

Jean-Pierre Vernant, *L'Individu, la mort, l'amour*,[4] Gallimard, collection Folio histoire, 1996.

Jean-Pierre Vernant, *L'Univers, les dieux, les hommes*,[5] Seuil, collection Points Essais, 2002.

Paul Veyne, *Les Grecs ont-ils cru à leurs mythes ?*,[6] Seuil, collection Points Essais, 1992.

---

3   TN: The History of Thought, Volume I.
4   TN: The Individual, Death and Love.
5   TN: The Universe, Gods and Men.
6   TN: Did the Greeks Believe Their Own Myths?

II

EXCELLENCE AS AN AIM

'To exist is to combat that which denies me.'

— DOMINIQUE VENNER (*The Rebel Heart*)

SIMULTANEOUSLY A PRIEST, A WARRIOR AND A PEASANT: TRIFUNCTIONALITY TODAY

BY OLIVIER EICHENLAUB

A T THE time when this book is being written, in the year of the Great Lockdown of 2020, a time when more than half of mankind has no other choice but to wage war against the most globalised — and therefore the most serious — pandemic of all time by quietly remaining at home, the various rifts inherent in capitalist societies are coming to light: there are those who wear masks and those who choose not to; those who have to go to work and those who can manage otherwise; and those who live in fear of their own downfall and those who know they will eventually pull through. Such rifts, however, are nothing new. Indeed, just a few months before the lockdown, these divisions had led to the revolt of the yellow vests, thus exposing the ruling oligarchy to the uprising of the *People of the Abyss*, to use the title of a book by Jack London, and laying bare the misery pervading 'peripheral France' in contrast with the privileged people inhabiting our gentrified metropolises and the untouchable ones residing in the ever-pampered suburbs. Nothing new under the sun, basically. Following the political angle initially formulated by Karl Marx, one which, in short, differentiates between the exploited proletariat and the members of the dominant bourgeoisie, Bourdieu[1] has analysed virtually the entire galaxy through the 'rich-vs-poor' prism, irremediably leaving little room for those who do have enough to get by but somehow count for nothing in today's logic, a logic that is still that of a perpetual class struggle rooted in conflict and rifts. There is seemingly nothing in Western democracies that could escape Sergio Leone's[2] masterfully synoptic slogan: 'You see, in this world there's two kinds of people, my friend: those with loaded guns and those who dig. You dig?' (*The Good, the Bad and the Ugly*, 1966).

Exiting This Rift-Based Society

Exiting this rift-based society requires one to combat its ubiquitous binary logic. In this regard, Stéphane Lupasco's[3] experimental work did look promising for a while. His line of thought, which he perceives as a generalisation of classical Aristotelian logic, aims to account for the tripolar becoming of matter-energy: macrophysical matter-energy, living matter-energy and psychological matter-energy, i.e. *The Three Types of Matter*, to use the title of his most famous book. The problem is that only few people have truly grasped Lupasco's logic, and none of those who believe themselves to have understood it has found any practical application for it in any field whatsoever, especially social sciences. Still, the fact remains that an opportunity has thus opened up, inviting us to revise our conception of both things and the world in harmony with a logic that is somewhat more complex than mere class or gender struggle.

---

1   TN: A prominent intellectual in several academic domains, Pierre Bourdieu (1930–2002) was a French sociologist.

2   TN: Sergio Leone (1929–1989) was an Italian film director most famous for having been a pioneer in the 'Spaghetti Western' genre.

3   TN: Born Ştefan Lupaşcu, Stéphane Lupasco (1900–1988) was a Romanian philosopher who developed what is known as non-Aristotelian logic.

In order to advance further, it is therefore preferable to go further back and re-examine the original mental structure of European civilisations, organised according to the trifunctional scheme highlighted by Georges Dumézil[4] when comparing Indo-European mythologies. Despite the very different political regimes and levels of organisation, the Greeks, Romans, Celts, Germans and Slavs abided by three essential orders that structured all social relations in accordance with a relatively balanced model: the first function, the sacerdotal one, is linked to sovereignty and the sacred; the second, that of the warrior, is connected with the defence of one's people; as for the third one, it is known as the production function and relates to fertility, and more generally to anything that makes it possible to build and develop an economy through work. To put things differently, *oratores* are men who, in traditional European societies, lead and pray for those who fight and work; *bellatores* are nobles who fight and defend the ones who pray and work, and *laboratores* are workers who provide those who pray or fight with food and equipment. Suffice to say that this system is not one of division and conflict but, on the contrary, one that is based on a complementarity created on all societal levels and stretching from symbolic mythological representations to the specific organisation of people's everyday lives. Had the expression not been corrupted in recent times, one could indeed speak of 'living together'.[5]

---

4   TN: A professor at the University of Istanbul, Georges Edmond Raoul Dumézil was a French philologist, linguist, religious studies scholar, and an expert in the field of comparative linguistics and mythology.

5   TN: The French expression *vivre ensemble*, i.e. 'living together', is used in reference to what is often termed 'diversity' in English. Under normal circumstances, the notion of 'living together' implies voluntary and harmonious co-existence, not the fact of being forced to accept the mass presence of foreign groups alongside your own — which is why the author describes the expression as having been corrupted.

In his *Poem to King Robert*, which was written around 1030 C.E.,
Adalbéron de Laon[6] expresses very clearly the unity and systemic
complementarity of the three Dumézilian functions:

> 'God's house, which we think of as one, is thus divided into three; some
> pray, others fight, and yet others work. The three groups, which coexist,
> cannot bear to be separated; the services rendered by one are a precondition
> for the labours of the two others; each in his turn takes it upon himself to
> relieve the whole. Thus the threefold assembly is none the less united.'

In its very theory, this model is therefore incompatible with both the
Marxist approach and the capitalist one, both of which are founded on
the exclusivity of economic determinants, determinants that reduce
the sacred and the art of war to utterly insignificant aspects, thereby
encouraging people to centre all social conflict solely around the tools
of economic production.

What of Trifunctionality, Then?

Encountered throughout the Indo-European world, this system remained widespread over time, with Georges Dumézil estimating that
trifunctionality had maintained its historical presence in Europe up
until the Estates General of 1789, when the clergy (the first function)
and nobility (the second function) voluntarily stepped aside before a
Third Estate (the third function) that has since constituted the new
economic and political elite, in accordance with the philosophy of the
Enlightenment. The French Revolution thus replaced the crown with
the wallets of those that were to comprise the plutocracy in power,
introducing hitherto unseen rifts among those that Karl Marx would
label the industrial bourgeoisie and the financial aristocracy (bankers,
the kings of stock markets, railroad magnates, and the owners of coal
and iron mines or forests): in all social spheres, 'the same prostitution

---

6   TN: Also known as Ascelin, Aldabéron de Laon was a French bishop and poet.

reproduced itself, the same shameless fraud, the same thirst to enrich oneself, not by production but by the filching of others' existing wealth.'

The situation has not improved much since Marx. On the contrary, it has asserted itself by erasing almost entirely the long centuries of structural heritage that Europe was founded on from Antiquity to the end of the Old Regime. What about the first function (the sovereign and sacerdotal one) in a world where the last remaining priests accumulate one moral scandal after another and have become the subject of jokes? Could it be that Islam, which is now on the verge of becoming the only true political religion of France, will, in the not too distant future, exercise a prayer monopoly over those who work and fight? And what about the second (war-related) function, with our soldiers being sent to support Uncle Sam in distant wars that no one wants nor understands, if, of course, they are not sick and tired of maintaining 'sentry' patrols that fight without any conviction whatsoever against a domestic terrorism that laughs in their face? The same goes for our police and gendarmerie forces, who, whether on the road or in the street, symbolise the truncheon of repression rather than the shield that protects widows and orphans. Last but not least, what about the third (production-related) function, at a time when agriculture has been modernised and financialised to the point where peasants, in the event that they have not yet committed suicide, are condemned to dutifully poison an entire population in small daily doses? And what about the rest of the population, kept busy by tertiary jobs that remain completely disconnected from all specific realities (David Graeber's[7] famous 'bullshit jobs'), with widespread burnout the ultimate career prospect? So many traumas and divisions that allow us to assess how far things have actually gone...

---

7   TN: In addition to being an anthropologist, American David Rolfe Graeber (12 February 1961 — 2 September 2020) was a famous anarchist activist.

Our Inner Empire

All is not lost, however, and we must trust Jean-Louis Garello's[8] words: indeed, trifunctionality is not merely a form of social organisation, but also a mental structure encountered among individuals, a thought pattern, a hierarchical system of values, and a manner in which one perceives both the world and themselves and that involves a 'harmonious relationship between three social authorities, three personal authorities, three brain levels'. He quotes Plato in order to demonstrate that society is divided in accordance with three functions, just as the soul of an individual is divided into three parts (his rational, irritable and productive sides) that allow one to distinguish the right from the left and the utopian from the tragic. In other words, we are all trifunctional by essence or heritage, within our own inner empire. We must not, therefore, capitulate. In the absence of a direct connection to the earth, it is necessary for us to re-learn how to 'experience' our landscapes beyond the superficial tours that characterise mass tourism, while also favouring the craftsmanship of a third function that provides us with a durable and comprehensive alternative to disposable trades and products. To use the figure of the warrior to complement the fundamental role of soldiers is to simultaneously become aware of the fact that the second function is also expressed through voluntary, political and collective activism and that it is necessary for us to fight 'against what denies us' (Dominique Venner) on a daily basis and regardless of the situation. Lastly, if we are to reclaim the first function, it is essential to cultivate a genuine local and functional subsidiarity and to rediscover our own Scriptures upon the stones of history. Such an updated implementation of the trifunctional model thus fits naturally into the historical trajectory of a long memory and struggle and should, in the long run, allow us to restore true social excellence, one that is free from all contemporary ideological disputes.

---

8   TN: Jean-Louis Garello is a French psychiatrist.

We can obviously see the problem coming from a mile away, as such solidarism based on historical trifunctionality is only made possible in the presence of a shared awareness of belonging to one single whole — the very same oneness mentioned by Adalbéron. Being part of one single whole is, however, only possible in a relatively homogeneous society. It goes without saying that this model is incompatible with the interchangeability of individuals imposed by the liberal and market ideology, and cannot be adapted to a population whose compliance with local requirements is very limited indeed or, worse, one that refuses to fulfil them with a view to imposing its own values instead. And it is here that we must bring up the fundamental lesson learnt from the Great Lockdown: we do have the means to reconnect with a certain kind of local solidarity, to applaud our everyday heroes, to no longer believe that constant roaming and travelling is a value in itself, and to understand that, in some cases, our jobs are utterly useless. The Great Lockdown will have at least enabled us to distinguish the fundamental from the futile and to differentiate between the necessary and the capricious. In such a context, it is no longer impossible to believe that the sustainability of deep-rooted and historically proven models can indeed counter the fluidity of artificial ideologies. More than ever before, the trifunctional model thus becomes, once again, a specificity that continues to resurface in the European mental structure, one that must permeate our awareness of the world by fuelling a tragic, and not utopian, perception of reality. For unlike those pre-chewed universalist ideologies, our reclaimed trifunctionality can obviously never guarantee the illusory advent of a bright future for all mankind. What it will do, however, is enable us to at least face the real world and channel its evolution towards what we have always been.

Bibliographical References

Jack London, *The People of the Abyss* (1903), translated by F. Postif and N. Mauberret as *Le Peuple d'en bas* and re-published in French by Phébus, collection Libretto, 1999.

Christophe Guilluy, *La France périphérique*,[9] Flammarion, 2014.

Stéphane Lupasco, *Les Trois Matières*,[10] Julliard, 1960.

Georges Dumézil, *Les dieux souverains des Indo-Européens*,[11] Gallimard, collection Bibliothèque des Sciences humaines, 1977.

Karl Marx, *Die Klassenkämpfe in Frankreich — 1848 bis 1850, 1850, Les Luttes de classes en France, 1848–1850 — Le 18 brumaire de Louis Bonaparte*,[12] reprint by Jean-Jacques Pauvert, collection Libertés, 1954.

David Graeber, *Bullshit Jobs: A Theory* (2018), translated by E. Roy as *Bullshit Jobs, Les Liens qui libèrent*, 2018.

Jean-Louis Garello, *Qu'est-ce que la Nation?*,[13] Carrefour de l'Horloge, online publication.

---

9   TN: Peripheral France.

10   TN: The Three Types of Matter.

11   TN: The Sovereign Gods of the Indo-Europeans.

12   TN: The Class Struggles in France, 1848–1850; The Eighteenth Brumaire of Louis Bonaparte.

13   TN: What Is a Nation?

MOS MAIORUM: EVERYDAY EXCELLENCE

BY THIBAUD CASSEL[1]

OR ANYONE looking for a personal development breviary, these pages will be a disappointment. Indeed, they advocate the opposite view to the cooking recipes applied to the development of the individual, this cadaverous worm of liberal disorder. A society of *developed* individuals will place over-inflated and vain monads alongside each other, but without raising any men. Ever biased, excellence invites the *new* man to embrace his emancipation while delivering him into the hands of nihilism, instead of demanding his perfectioning in the interest of order — which is but the social name given to beauty.

What could be more bountiful than the millions of daily lives that constitute the very life of a people? They are united by countless interactions and a community of destiny; for the very art of living conjugates in the plural. Even a hermit prays for the world — by contrast, liberal chaos limits our adventurous exploits to the resources provided by our credit card… While the atomised individual is accounted for by the market, a deep-rooted man can only be accounted for by the community in which his existence acquires its very meaning. From where we stand, the challenge that we face in our everyday lives amounts

---

1   TN: Thibaud Cassel is a French author who has worked for various European institutions in Brussels.

to keeping all pernicious tendencies in check by making individuality yield to uses that actually exalt it.

To Stand to Attention Is to Take Action

Let us be careful not to fall into the trap of mere *posture*, where one impeccably stands to attention only to conceal the false ethics of sheer appearances. Indeed, to stand to attention is to take action — as it should be. Let us also dismiss the vague mystique of adventure. When adopted as a code of conduct, the fact of always being *at odds with things* or *avoiding them* limits one's existence to the level of teenager games. The adventure that life undoubtedly is consists in understanding the laws that govern us and excelling in this regard. If a fiery sort of youth prevents a people's teeth from chattering, its members cannot thrive in fever. Isn't that, in fact, the symmetrical opposite of the morbid apathy in which we are now wallowing? In line with a holistic approach, to have a good life is to earn one's merit within the collective structures of the family and community — both of which are organic categories of the people. If prodigious individuals and heroes can exist, collective life is a rather favourable environment to foster their emergence. The birth of an artist's genius presupposes the presence of other artists among whom he excels. He and his peers will organise themselves into an association or corporation, that is to say a community, just like a plant whose flower expresses its genius.

In short, it is a matter of naturally championing excellence, so that we may fulfil our obligations amidst the determinisms that elevate us, while we ourselves act as a determinism that elevates others. This organised aspect of our everyday lives has come to us from afar; for it is quite reminiscent of the *Works and Days* of the Greek poet Hesiod. Wisdom teaches us how to live a good life, a life that will ultimately be crowned with greatness. For it is then that the value of the individual can develop freely. Indeed, there is an essential saying that stems from Greek wisdom and that calls for such understanding — *'know thyself'* can thus be explained exactly as follows: 'know thy place in the (familial, political, cosmic or religious) order of things'.

Today, perpetuating Delphic wisdom requires one to have the right understanding of the times that we are going through. The ancient code of ethics that we are formulating proceeds from the state of severe disintegration afflicting Western nations, where the community sphere now flourishes in the gap that separates the individual from the nation. Just like excellence, the community has thus been undermined. Faced with the general disaffiliation which our contemporaries are now experiencing, the individual's need for collective belonging can only be channelled through his rallying to a minority cause. These active minorities thus form small structured cells in order to escape the pain of living among the anonymous, shapeless and compliant majority. Following a scavenger's instincts, they lay down their own foundations so as to better distance themselves from this shared fate. Such a rout is obviously repulsive to all noble hearts. Consistency in commitment cannot, however, be left to chance. Instead, it adheres to the unavoidably collective dimension of all human life.

On the contrary, an accomplished man acknowledges himself as a member of the majority, that of his people, sharing its torments in the face of relegation, obliteration and degradation. He does not defend the people, but rather embodies the people defending themselves; indeed, he proclaims what to the majority is but a vague feeling, and above all, commits himself where others simply resign. He is thus not above but at the very heart of the people. To shoulder responsibility 'so that the golden light of dawn may mirror that of sunset' — such is the *raison d'être* of every elite community; of every aristocracy, in other words. The central role of individuality defines the very European character of such ethics. For what characterises us is the notion of equivalence between responsibility and freedom, where other civilisations confine man to leading an inner life, embracing worldly detachment or accepting the inevitability of fate. As stated by Saint-Exupéry,[2] 'to be a man is, precisely, to be responsible. [...] It is to feel, when setting one's stone, that one is contributing to the building of the world'.

Each person's abilities assign certain responsibilities to them. In accordance with an immutable social law, each and every vulnerability is subject to discipline and all power stems from solidarity. Such is the case of the family, which the father protects and commands. As for the mother, it is she who gives life and thus epitomises the primary human power, acting as the guardian of traditions in the household. The community itself is to be seen as a family of families, one where all social diversity finds its rightful place. Each trade and each social function encourages excellence, for a living society is akin to the cosmos, ever a constellation of aristocracies. Last but not least, let us be rid of the prejudices connected with the term 'elite'. A rural community or Greek city is elitist insofar as it perceives itself as being free and responsible. For their part, the mighty may only act as the vectors or annuitants of decomposition. Faced with the stranglehold imposed by the Leviathan-State and current technology, the quest for independence must be pursued outside all romantic reveries and obsolete forms.

Constructing Our World

The community paves the way towards a noble life, along a path that man must travel as far as he can. In the age of mediaeval Christianity, the path led to man's salvation; in today's liberal West, it leads to the hoarding of wealth. Having once been savable, man has now become soluble— and a source of profit. The triumph of the individual required the sacrificing of the people, a people now left massified, objectified and disfigured. In contrast with this, the very meaning of a committed daily life and of all individual excellence now depends on our

---

2   TN: Known as Antoine de Saint-Exupéry, Antoine Marie Jean-Baptiste Roger, comte de Saint-Exupéry (1900–1944), was a French author, poet, aristocrat, journalist and pioneering aviator.

adherence to ensuring the continuity of our people; on our keeping the promise that we shall neither be erased nor replaced.

To escape the serfdom imposed by the Polish lords, Slavic peasants organised themselves into an independent community in the outer reaches of Europe, where no state exercised its authority: the Cossacks thus emerged. For centuries, they would play the role of Slavic and Christian *limes* in the face of the Muslim Orient before being used in the Russian conquest of lands that stretched from the Caucasus all the way to the Pacific Ocean. With the collapse of the Western Roman Empire, many Italians would retreat to the inhospitable lagoons located to the north of the peninsula and build Venice, which foreshadowed, and served as both model and vector for, their embryonic civilisation. From our perspective as well, the community establishes itself as a source of secession or even an act of war, as conflict is indeed the foundation of everything. On closer examination, however, our hostility is directed against all that is dead within society, and the allure of identity is such that the community conjoins with society in its living aspects.

In other words, the communitarianism that we support is to be understood as a ruse devised by the people to regain strong support. It allows to harmonise thought and action before transforming our actions into a living thought. It offers one the opportunity to live a full life rather than to cultivate noble ideas in the unproductive soil of servile living conditions. The initial scope of a dissident daily life reflects the following slogan: 'You must live in accordance with your own thoughts — otherwise, you will end up shaping your thoughts in accordance with your own life'. Its ultimate scope, however, involves the establishment and foreshadowing of a society to come. In the words of Ernst Jünger,[3] 'creation is not an initial act: it is possible at any point where the flames of the unexpected burn. Bonding with one another is

---

3   TN: Ernst Jünger (1895–1998) was a German writer, highly decorated soldier, philosopher, and entomologist known for his World War I memoir entitled *Storm of Steel*.

not just the goal of love, but that of all superior communions, whatever their nature.'

This century denies all that we are—the only way to exist in it without submitting to it is thus to resist it. And the only way to emerge victorious is to create spaces that keep chaos away. This is not a time to retreat along the banks of the Dnieper. Our present struggle, *hic et nunc*, keeps the people warm through its bonfires: with every child to be born, with every awakened memory, and with each and every blow aimed at whoever would deny us.

Mos Maiorum

Alongside general perspectives, it is necessity that represents the second painting of the diptych; for circumstances fuel existence beyond good and evil. An honorable daily life could never be an intricate one, since our ancestors embraced it within the humbleness of their own peasant lives. It is, in fact, both simple and challenging, just like harvesting wheat or climbing a mountain. Having said that, the more prosaic pieces of advice cannot be part of a caricatural list akin to the one in Prévert's[4] poem. Indeed, it is not a matter of formulating religious precepts. The pious ambition of 'knowing oneself' does, however, give us some clues. Everyone can assess their own situation by answering the following fundamental questions: where? When? What? How? These question marks can be used in conjunction with the Roman values that bestowed upon the City its worldly rights: the *mos maiorum*.

Where will I live? I can't claim nature as my foundation while thriving in the urban jungle; nor can I disdain commercial disorder while savouring industrial abundance — such is the lesson that frugality (*frugalitas*) teaches us. As for constance (*constantia*), it urges me to rediscover the meaning of long-term endeavours, despite the erratic current events that I bestride. Yet it is now that I am required to give

---

4   TN: Jacques Prévert (1900–1977) was a French poet and screenwriter. One of his most famous poems is actually written in the form of a list.

of my life. And this is where one of the parameters of my situation comes in to modify another: indeed, virtue (*virtus*) commands me not to yield the first line of defence under any circumstances. Fortunately, gravity (*gravitas*) protects me against the acid that corrodes this 'spectacle society'. I reflect on the degree to which sneering debases the majesty (*majestas*) of the people, a majesty that determines the extent to which I fail to find any human grandeur outside those attitudes that contribute to collective greatness. Through my profession or the function that I fulfil, I add my own stone to the collective work. No matter how heavy it is, I feel light when taking it on. Never frustrating in the slightest, such an effort allows me to grow, so strong the piety (*pietas*) that binds me to the deities that answer my pleas by exalting me. Last but not least, my fidelity (*fides*) with regard to the commitments I make ensures that I am always there to lend my loved ones a helping hand, just as they themselves are in my time of need.

These principles are both demanding enough to keep us in line and general enough to apply to us all. They outline the archway towards which we can all strive with confidence, as it will not fall on our heads. Indeed, these ribbed vaults draw their strength from their dynamic relationship. When abiding by such laws, man contributes to invigorating the living aspects of society. For the word *fides* has resulted in the French words *fidelité* and *foi*,[5] i.e. in one of the three Christian theological virtues alongside hope and charity, which represent further virtues that one must have, not only because they inspired those of our ancestors who built this country, but also because they possess a power that we cannot deny. These virtues are ours, regardless of where we source them from.

In his book entitled *Un samouraï d'Occident*,[6] Dominique Venner, whose conduct was particularly exemplary, makes a few recommendations that suit this conclusion perfectly. He recommends that we foster

---

5   TN: Faithfulness and faith.

6   TN: A Samurai of the West.

a close relationship with nature, whether through hunting trips or walks. He also enjoins us to practise some kind of martial art in order to cultivate a specific type of virility, especially since such disciplines bring together individuals whose taste for effort is still very much present. Last but not least, he urges us to write often and re-read our texts, so as to nurture our awareness of our own actions.

Bibliographical References

Dominique Venner, *Un samouraï d'Occident — Le bréviaire des insoumis,* Pierre-Guillaume de Roux, 2013.

THE AGE OF THE *OPUS* — TO RID OURSELVES OF THE IDEOLOGY OF WORK

BY ALIX MARMIN[1]

THERE IS NO life without work! 'To man, living has always been synonymous with working', claimed the philosopher Michel Henry. If this is indeed the case, how are we to explain the contradictions characterising the demands of our age? On the one hand, productivity, performance, and efficiency; on the other, the quest for well-being, recentring, and personal and professional fulfilment. In truth, this apparent discrepancy is but an illusion, as happiness has simply become a production factor like any other, one that must be maximised. If companies tend to interfere in our lives, it is simply because capitalism is an omnivorous entity: it consumes anything that helps it grow, continuing to do so until it succeeds in governing even the smallest aspects of the lives of its 'salaried employees'. Indeed, it is well-aware of the fact that if happiness is injected in small doses, the worker or employee will be more motivated, more efficient, and thus a better source of profit. Ubiquitous, work imposes itself as the value of values, one that has an essential economic and social impact.

---

1   TN: With a solid education in the field of art history, Alix Marmin is an author who writes for the French bi-monthly magazine *Éléments*.

What work do we mean, however? When reflecting on its evolution, the mistake would be that of projecting onto it the role and value that our time and age assign to it. On the contrary, at a time when *bullshit jobs* are flourishing (those superficial and socially irrelevant jobs that capitalise on useless and meaningless tasks), it seems essential to us to radically redefine our relationship to work and thus revert to its very essence. Putting things into perspective on a historical level will allow us to reflect on the concept of work, having re-situated it in the wider context of the action-contemplation dyad, in harmony with a radically European and contemporary worldview.

Otium and *Negotium*

Work has not always been man's primary activity. In traditional, primitive and ancient civilisations, work was generally a stigma. A sign of social and moral inferiority, and unworthy of a good citizen, it was associated with a state of enslavement and submission to a master. It was regarded as a constraint arising from necessity, especially the material kind, and experienced as an inevitability. Indeed, freedom was only conceivable when exempt from this necessity, beyond the economic sphere. In his *Mythe et pensée chez les Grecs*,[2] historian and anthropologist Jean-Pierre Vernant highlights, at the end of a semantic analysis, the differences in work valorisation: in Ancient Greek, there is no single word that would serve as an equivalent to our generic and comprehensive term 'work'; instead, there are several, according to the particularities and purposes of each activity (craft-related, technical, agricultural, etc.). Work was not understood as — nor unified into — one single concept, but subordinated to realities that were deemed superior, including ethics or politics. Restricted to the familial domain, i.e. to the private sphere, the *oikonomia* thus applied above all to the *oikos* (household) in the broad sense of the term, that is to say to the family, its slaves and its material possessions. By contrast,

2   TN: Greek Myth and Thought.

social and public life acquired its meaning outside the field of work, in the community's most significant events such as celebrations, games, ceremonies, and war.

Work has not always held sway over contemplation. The Romans thus distinguished between *labor*, defined as arduous and painful work, and *opus*, which referred to (a) completed work. Whereas the former is reactive and often passive, the latter is, on the contrary, active, enabling the expression of a certain will. The Latin word *otium* is a concept inspired by the Greek *skhole* and referring to the free time that one dedicates to study and meditation, to fruitful leisure time allowing one to meditate and reflect on things. When misused, *otium* can take on a negative and unwanted form, causing slow-wittedness or laxness. This flaw had already been denounced in Antiquity, and traces of this pejorative meaning have survived in the word '*idleness*'. In its noble meaning, *otium* was glorified by Cicero, Seneca, and many Stoic authors, all of whom considered it to be the necessary condition for any action, in contrast with agitation and busyness, i.e. *negotium*. An accomplished man does not differentiate between action and contemplation and bears within himself the will to educate himself intellectually.

The purpose of work has not always been one of utility and profitability (see chapter 9). In his work on mediaeval economy, Guillaume Travers[3] mentioned a society in which professions were not only limited to utilitarian and commercial considerations. Trade communities (guilds, trade associations) are, therefore, genuine living communities: they give everyday life its own rhythm and are part of social and religious existence. Thus, each trade association has its own patron saint, its own festivals, and also its own rules and traditions. In *L'Argent*,[4] Charles Péguy[5] speaks of a time when people gave the best

---

3   TN: Guillaume Travers is a French writer whose works and articles often focus on the topic of ecology.

4   TN: Money.

5   TN: Charles Pierre Péguy (1873–1914) was a French poet, essayist and editor.

of themselves in their work, which allowed them to find fulfilment and attain self-realisation: 'When work is established as an absolute, one quickly becomes a poor worker. Indeed, one's love of a job done well does not stem from their fondness of work itself, but from their love of perfection. It is, in fact, of metaphysical origin.' In this respect, the construction of cathedrals during the prosperous European 12th and 13th centuries is an example from which one can truly learn a lot. Having studied the manner in which cathedrals were financed, Henry Kraus[6] demonstrated that the choice to dedicate all excess wealth to this purpose rather than channel it towards other monetary and commercial items would have been deemed meaningless in a society that valued only utility and profitability.

The Ideology of Work

Work is valorised as an ideology. Indeed, the modern conception of work stems from capitalist production and economic growth. As for philosopher André Gorz, he describes work as an 'activity belonging to the public sphere, one that is requested, defined, and acknowledged to be useful by others, who thus remunerate you for it'. Acting as a socialisation factor, work conditions our very integration into modern society and determines our worth. Its hegemonic authority would have us believe that it cannot be viewed differently, which is why Jacques Ellul perceives it as an ideological phenomenon that has permeated every stratum of society and, to a large extent, dominated our mentalities. He thus analyses the convergence of four Western trends that fostered the birth of the 'ideology of work': the ever-increasing difficulty in working conditions, which had to be justified by means of an ideology that presented it as a virtue; the relinquishment of traditional values and beliefs; the cult of economic growth, now defined as an absolute value; and the separation between those who command and those who obey.

---

6   TN: Henry Kraus (1906–1995) was a European art historian and labour historian.

Work has become an abstract activity. Globalisation has led to the disappearance of structuring standards and reference points, to an absence of direction: loss of one's sense of reality, complexification, the geographic fragmentation of production processes, virtualisation, etc. We thus find ourselves unable to define the purposes that give our work meaning. It is all, furthermore, a consequence of management ideology, which has now been raised to the level of scientific discipline by so-called 'coaches' and made sacred by 'consultants' and other charlatans that specialise in the running of organisations. This ideology has proceeded to glorify 'human resources' (HR) in what is but a hollow and inflated type of newspeak, as company work becomes a genuine way of life, and employees a resource, a capital to be managed and profited from, and, above all, 'men with no inner dimension'. For a company worthy of its name, human ressources are essential, having insidiously modified the very meaning of work by resorting to words that are as enticing as they are soothing: 'the development of your creativity, autonomy and well-being'.

Work has ceased to be a part of life (in the strong sense). Instead, it invades and devours the latter to become a mere means to earn one's living (in the weak sense): a necessary activity allowing one to obtain money, live off this money and finance one's hobbies. The Greeks thus used two different terms, a weak and a strong one, to refer to life: *zoe*, which expressed the simple fact of being alive, and *bios*, a way of life that is specific to a certain individual or group. Ultimately, work has been gaining an increasingly important position in people's everyday lives, perhaps even the most pre-eminent one. It is so difficult to resist the constant demand for flexibility, production and consumption that their working hours are getting longer in an almost natural manner, with their needs growing ever more numerous. This phenomenon is exacerbated by the increasing importance of the digital domain, which makes 'disconnection' even more difficult. What about all those pensioners who feel useless once they have stopped working and no longer find any purpose or meaning in their lives? Having lived to work, their state of mind stems from the triumph of the 'ideology of work' and from their own failure to unite life and work into one single whole.

The Reward of Rewards

When separated from life and regarded as a means to an end, work is no longer appreciated for what it is, but rather for what it offers, for the advantages that it brings. Friedrich Nietzsche refused to bestow upon wealth and profit a value of their own, calling for a sovereign kind of work, one whose purpose does not extend beyond it and from which we derive pleasure. After all, should life not be the driving force behind our actions, words and thoughts? Instead of embracing the fallacious contradiction between work and life, one had better advocate the union of these two notions into a homogeneous, coherent and harmonious whole that will allow people to develop the gift of self-sacrifice and self-realisation in the face of the disillusionment caused by a contemporary world devoid of values. To control one's existence and give one's life and activities their long lost meaning is, in harmony with Nietzsche's precepts, to become men that 'are choosy, hard to satisfy, and do not care for ample rewards, if the work itself is not to be the reward of rewards'.

The disappearance of *otium* leads to cultural and civilisational decline. Anything that might slow down the production and consumption pace, especially contemplation in its positive and traditional sense, thus inevitably disappears: the praise of beauty, commitment to city affairs and contemplation as defined by Aristotle are thus all relinquished. For modern man 'has no time' for contemplation, silence, and inner stillness, all of which are necessary for a 'good and righteous' life. There is, however, no need to choose between these two states. Let us therefore rediscover our taste for such higher and more rewarding activities! Let us also restore our taste for effort through manual work, which, according to Jean-Jacques Rousseau, dips our soul into the river Styx, as it teaches us to anticipate and foresee things, as well as to 'reconcile, compare and establish relationships either from a practical perspective or with a useful end in view'. Action and Contemplation indeed. So how about granting our conception of work a new value that is not separate from but consubstantial with life itself?

Bibliographical References

Michel Henry, *Réinventer la culture*,[7] Le Monde des débats, September 1993.

David Graeber, *Bullshit Jobs: A Theory*, 2018, translated by E. Roy as *Bullshit Jobs, Les Liens qui libèrent*, 2018.

Jean-Pierre Vernant, *Mythe et pensée chez les Grecs — Études de psychologie historique*, La Découverte, collection Poche / Sciences humaines et sociales, 2005.

Guillaume Travers, *Économie médiévale et société féodale*,[8] La Nouvelle Librairie, collection Longue Mémoire de l'Institut Iliade, 2020.

Henry Kraus, *L'Argent des cathédrales*,[9] CNRS / Cerf, collection Biblis, 2012.

André Gorz, *Métamorphoses du travail*,[10] Galilée, 1991.

Jacques Ellul (P. Mendès), *L'idéologie du travail*.[11] *Foi et Vie*, issue number 4, July 1980.

Jean-Pierre Le Goff, *Les Illusions du management — Pour le retour du bon sens*,[12] La Découverte, collection Poche / Essais, 2003.

Friedrich Nietzsche, *Die fröhliche Wissenschaft*,[13] 1882. Translated from German by P. Wotling, *Le Gai Savoir*, Flammarion, collection GF, 2007.

Jean-Jacques Rousseau, *Émile ou De l'éducation*,[14] Gallimard, collection Folio, 1969.

---

7   TN: Reinventing Culture.

8   TN: Mediaeval Economy and Feudal Society.

9   TN: Cathedral Funding.

10 TN: Work Metamorphoses.

11 TN: The Ideology of Work.

12 TN: The Delusions of Management — For a Return of Common sense.

13 TN: The Joyful Science.

14 TN: Emile, or On Education.

FOR A EUROPEAN REBIRTH — RESTORING THE THREAD OF CONTINUITY

BY JEAN-YVES LE GALLOU[1]

'Co-existence' and 'living-together'—such is the ordinance that Europeans are to abide by at the start of the 21st century. We are to 'live together' with people we have nothing in common with in terms of origin, mores, customs, prohibitions, religion and civilisation. Such is, however, the order issued in all European countries in a desire to achieve 'diversity': either in the name of multiculturalism, as seen in Great Britain, the Scandinavian countries, Germany and Belgium, or, as witnessed in France, on the basis of a distorted conception of assimilation, which has now turned into 'integration' and 'inclusion'. All against the backdrop of an inversion in the very severity of constraints imposed, on the one hand, on natives, and on the other, on those that have come from elsewhere. The usual requirement where immigrants were asked to adapt to the rules of the host country has now been relinquished, thus making cohabitation even more difficult. Consequently, in order to make this increasingly conflictual 'co-existence' possible, the progressive elites have introduced

---

1   TN: Born in 1948, Jean-Yves Le Gallou is a French politician and a former member of the European Parliament.

a formidable mechanism intended to deconstruct traditions, history, and cultural and religious reference points. The purpose is to convince people that there is no past and no future, no men and no women, no whites and no blacks, and neither Christians nor non-Christians. Globalist oligarchs have renounced all attempts to acculturate others, preferring to uproot our natives instead. The Great Upheaval is thus used to the benefit of the Great Replacement. The Great Erasure of our memory paves the way for the Great Replacement of our peoples in an unprecedented sort of development.

A Clear Line since the Dawn of Greek Civilisation

For despite any historical divergences, the history of Europeans is characterised by an unbroken continuity reaching back to the dawn of Greek civilisation, and by a series of rebirths involving a return to our very roots. It was Renan who drew our attention to this fact in his famous lecture of 1882, one that is often misinterpreted as a negation of the very role of origins and entitled 'What Is a Nation?'. In its simplicity, the famous Spartan chant 'We are what you were; we shall be what you are!' is the abridged anthem of every fatherland. Although the Athenians, Spartans, Thebans, Aeginatans, Milesians and the citizens of other cities did not think of themselves as Greeks, they knew they were all Hellenic when facing barbarians. They managed to unite against the great Persian king before submitting to Macedonian and, later on, Roman domination.

What followed was the first stage of the long European continuity: the now-vanquished Greece bequeathed its epics to the Romans (the *Iliad* and the *Odyssey*, which inspired the *Aeneid*), in addition to its mythology and metamorphoses, its philosophy (Plato, Aristotle, Marcus Aurelius, Lucretius), its mathematics and astronomy, its rhetoric, and its art (sculpture in particular). The Roman elites were bilingual and spoke Greek as well as Latin. Rome expanded its dominion to include the entire Mediterranean (*Mare nostrum*), from the Euxine Sea (the

Black Sea) to the Pillars of Hercules (the Strait of Gibraltar). Roman law and organisation thus spread through these areas, as did the Greek culture. At the dawn of the 1st century, Octavian, one of the greatest statesmen in history, founded a political structure that would last for four centuries; even longer, when one considers its distant heir, the Holy Roman Empire, which lasted until 1806. And perhaps even until today, through the notion of empire, which remains very present in Europe.

During the 4th century, divisions and rifts increased, as barbarians defied Roman borders and political instability set in. The old Roman religion began to decline, and Christianity prevailed. Grief-stricken, the old Romans (Celsus, Ammianus Marcellinus, Symmachus) watched the world of the *mos maiorum* (the ancestral code of conduct) crumble. Even today, the fall of the Roman Empire remains a topic to be pondered.

A Historical Path Lined with Rebirths

Regardless of any divisions, however, it is most often continuity that prevails. Born of a Jewish sect, Christianity is quickly Hellenised. The Gospels are translated and written in Greek. Greek philosophy and myths fuel what is hence to be called Helleno-Christianity. Having been educated in the field of Latin rhetoric, Christian authors such as Tertullian and Augustine of Hippo take over from Cicero, Seneca and Livy to reflect on the great Roman figures, including Regulus, who went from victorious hero to unfortunate protagonist of the first Punic War. A Roman general and consul during the First Punic War, Regulus would seize Tunis in 255 B.C. A stroke of bad luck would, however, then lead to Roman defeat. Having been taken prisoner, he is instructed by the Carthaginians to communicate their peace proposals to Rome, proposals which he advises the Roman Senate not to accept. Faithful to his own word, he then returns and surrenders himself as a prisoner to Carthage, where he is tortured and put to death. His story and attitude have fuelled the reflections of philosophers, apologists and theologians alike.

The relationship that ties the empire to Christianity is twofold. Indeed, primitive Christianity is often considered a source of dissolution of Roman society. Following the collapse of the Western Roman Empire, however, it was the Church that extended the latter's existence by taking charge of its organisation and territorial structures, as bishops replaced prefects. When, in 496, Clovis renounced paganism to worship 'Clotilde's god', he opted for Catholic orthodoxy, which guaranteed him the support of the bishops, rather than Arianism, a heresy that denied the consubstantiality of the Father and the Son, and was quite popular among Germanic converts. Once again, this epitomised a type of imperial continuity.

As for the history of the Middle Ages, it was punctuated with rebirths, i.e. with instances where one returned to their roots: examples include the Carolingian Renaissance, the Ottonian Renaissance, and the Renaissance of the 12th century. At the time when they still existed, the good textbooks that dealt with French history presented Charlemagne as the inventor of schools. It was all but a figurative way to refer to the Carolingian renaissance: the renewal of studies, the presence of the educated at the royal court, the development of libraries, the revival of the Latin language and its writings, and the cultivation of liberal arts: *trivium* (grammar, dialectics, rhetoric) and *quadrivium* (arithmetic, music, geometry, astronomy). This revival is, however, contested by some historians, who assert that there was no intermission during the [alleged] 'dark ages' that lasted from the 5th to the 8th century. Nevertheless, it was in Rome, at Christmas time in 800 C.E., that the coronation of Charlemagne took place, thus re-founding the empire.

Occuring two centuries later, it is the Ottonian Renaissance that must be mentioned, a period that had its own great intellectuals (such as Gerbert d'Aurillac, the pope of the year one thousand) and artistic revival, whether in terms of its churches, palaces or illuminated manuscripts. This enlightenment came from the Roman Empire of the East, thanks to Empress Theophano, the Byzantine princess and wife of Otto II. Greek language and thought re-emerged as great Byzantine-inspired churches were built. Having miraculously evaded the Anglo-American bombardments of the Second World War, the capital of the Ottonian Empire, Quedlinburg, remains, ten centuries later, a jewel of mediaeval and Renaissance architecture.

A further two centuries would pass before the Renaissance of the 12th century, which acted as a prelude to the *Age of Cathedrals* and to the great theological discussions regarding both Thomism and nominalism. In a book that outraged bigoted minds, Sylvain Gouguenheim demonstrated that the abbey of Mont-Saint-Michel had welcomed experts who translated Aristotle directly from Greek into Latin, without having to go through Syriac and Arabic, as claimed by the Islamophilic ideology. Throughout Europe, the spread of these translations of ancient texts that had come to us directly from Constantinople, without the need for any detours through *al-Andalus*, was considerable. It thus inspired Bernard of Chartres[2] (around 1100 C.E.) to express the following thought:

> We are like dwarfs on the shoulders of giants, so that we can see more than they, and things at a greater distance, not by virtue of any sharpness of sight on our part, or any physical distinction, but because we are carried high and raised up by their giant size.

A most powerful statement indeed, one that was later adopted by Newton when highlighting the fundamental role of transmission.

The Fall of Constantinople

1453 is a key date in history, as the world witnesses the fall of both Constantinople and the Eastern Roman Empire. In the eyes of many

---

2   TN: Born in Brittany, France, Bernard of Chartres was a French scholar, administrator and philosopher.

historiographers, it heralds the end of the Middle Ages and the beginning of the great Renaissance. In reality, the origin of the ancient texts that centre around the West reaches much further back in time than the conquest of Byzantium at the hands of the Turks. And it is the Italian Quattrocento that marks the beginning of the Renaissance. The fact remains, however, that the fall of Constantinople accelerated this transmission and acculturation by driving many Byzantine scholars to take refuge in Italy. Through sculpture, painting, and literature, Antiquity makes a strong comeback in the art and mind-set of the European world. As regards painting, it is portraiture and the acknowledgement of the uniqueness of every person that thrive, as large-scale paintings — ones that focus on history or mythology, both of which were inherited from Antiquity — take on a growing importance that rivals that of religious paintings. This great prosperity would then be extended further by classical and baroque art.

Preceded by The Crisis of the European Mind (1685–1715), the advent of the Enlightenment causes Europe to plummet towards modernity. Until 1750, the issue of identity had not come up: indeed, every man was regarded as belonging to a certain place, as the product of a given heritage. And this was generally the case with religion as well, all in accordance with the following principle applied in Germany: *cujus regio, ejus religio* ('Whose land, his religion'). And it was the Enlightenment that raised the issue of 'constructed' identity by freeing man from his naturalness in the name of free choice. Immediately afterwards, the American and French revolutions proceeded to emancipate subjects from the power of monarchs, associations, states and their own cultural and religious heritage. For better or for worse.

The ammunition wagons of the Great Revolution awakened the national sentiments of our peoples, for the 19th century was that of nationalities. From 1789 to 1945, the issue of identity is addressed within the sole reductive framework of nations, without the notion of empire ever disappearing: we thus had the French Empire (under Napoleon I and Napoleon III); the Austrian Empire (heir to the Holy Empire); and the Russian Empire, which regarded Moscow as the third Rome, one that was now carrying the torch of Constantinople.

And it was the disaster of 1914–1918 that led to contemporary nihilism. Indeed, industrial warfare discredits heroic values. The Treaty of Versailles created the necessary conditions for the next disaster, with national identity disintegrating after 1945. Propped against the condemnation of National Socialism, Germany's guilt is gradually extended to all European nations, and soon enough to the denunciation of colonialism and slavery, which Europeans — unlike all other peoples — had actually abolished. Instead of a history that puts great exploits into perspective without ever disregarding the paths less travelled, one instils into Europeans an adulterated and destructive 'duty of rememberance' in which the continuity of both European history and its values seems forever lost.

Restoring the Thread of Continuity

If what they want is to leave their mark upon the commencing century, and not end up in the wastebins of history, Europeans must pull themselves together and regenerate themselves. They must transcend the age of division (1789, 1945, 1968) and renew the thread of continuity by becoming conscious of, acknowledging and proudly embracing their own ethnic, civilisational and religious origins. The population of Europe, taken in its unchanged form that lasted until the mid-20th century, is actually 5,000 years old, going back to a time when the original European people began their diaspora upon departing the Pontic steppes towards the east and Siberia; towards the south, Persia and India; and especially towards the west, that is to say Europe. The men and women who were part of the corded ware culture thus gradually occupied Western Europe, a mostly uninhabited land with the exception of a small number of hunter-gatherers with whom the Indo-European conquerors merged. And therein lies the ethnic foundation of the European people.

Not to mention the origin of European civilisation — that of its languages (Slavic, Germanic, Celtic, and Roman), all of which have a common origin, including their vocabulary and syntax. This also accounts for the shared cosmogony and for a specific social organisation centred around hierarchy and a distinction between the functions of (magical-religious) sovereignty, (domestic and foreign) defence, and production and reproduction; in addition to a notion of the world based on representation and incarnation, as well as on the respect one owes to women. In order to protect their own space, continent and world, Europeans had to fight against the outside world: the West thus clashed with the East, as the Greek notions of freedom triumphed over the Persian Empire, Roman reason over Carthage, and the Romans and their barbarian allies over the Hunnic hordes that had come from Asia to the Catalaunian Plains. Next, for fourteen long centuries, Christianity and Islam would clash as part of the *Reconquista* of the Iberian Peninsula, the Crusades and the fight against the Great Turk. It would also be correct to speak of the Christian identity of Europe, one that resulted from the union between the Gospel message, Roman reason and Greek thought; from a coupling of scholarly culture and popular faith, thus glorifying a sacred and age-old geography and achieving harmony between sky and roots.

For what is a people? It's the fact of having common origins, a shared geography, a similarly organised space, and common interests; which Europeans undoubtedly do. And the requirements set by Renan are all within our reach: 'To have common glories in the past, a common will in the present; to have done great things together; to wish to do greater; these are the essential conditions which make up a people'.

And as stated by Dominique Venner, 'Europe was not born of the agreements signed at the end of the 20th century; it stems from brotherly peoples who, from the Baltic to the Aegean, gave birth, over a period of a few millennia, to an unequalled community of culture'. It is thus time — high time — Europeans reclaimed their own heritage, seeking regeneration in high places, sublime landscapes, great museums, the wealth of libraries, the lives of illustrious men, and the memories of great deeds.

Bibliographical References

Thibaud Cassel et Henri Levavasseur, *L'idée impériale en Europe*,[3] published in *Ce que nous sommes*. Collective work, Pierre-Guillaume de Roux, collection Institut Iliade, 2018.

Yvan Blot, *L'Héritage d'Athéna — Les racines grecques de l'Occident*,[4] Les Presses bretonnes, 1996.

Georges Duby, *Le Temps des cathédrales — L'Art et la société (980–1420)*,[5] Gallimard, collection Bibliothèque des Histoires, 1976.

Sylvain Gouguenheim, *Aristote au Mont Saint-Michel — Les racines grecques de l'Europe chrétienne*,[6] Seuil, collection l'Univers historique, 2008.

Paul Hazard, *La Crise de la conscience européenne*,[7] Boivin et Cie, 1935.

---

3   TN: The Imperial Notion in Europe.

4   TN: Athena's Legacy — The West's Greek Roots.

5   TN: The Age of Cathedrals — Art and Society.

6   TN: Aristotle on Mont Saint-Michel — The Greek Roots of Christian Europe.

7   TN: The Crisis of the European Mind.

III

BEAUTY AS OUR HORIZON

'We are entering a time when words
will have to be validated by actions.'

— Dominique Venner, *La manif du 26 mai et Heidegger*[1]

---

1   TN: The Protests of 26 May and Heidegger.

BEYOND BOURGEOIS UTILITARIANISM — RE-ENCHANTING THE WORLD

BY GUILLAUME TRAVERS

M ODERN MAN'S relation to the surrounding world is an almost exclusively utilitarian one. Faced with every single thing, he wonders whether it is of value to him, whether it satisfies any of his desires, and whether it can contribute to his personal comfort. In his eyes, a tradition is only worth preserving insofar as it provides him with pleasure and amusement — he thus breaks with it as soon as it turns out to be burdensome. In accordance with this same logic, everything is subject to comparative evaluation in terms of its costs and benefits: a natural landscape can therefore be destroyed if building a block of flats instead proves financially profitable. Everything is a matter of 'good business'. Utilitarian man thus only exists as a perpetual consumer of goods, all of which can be purchased and sold. Nothing has any intrinsic value to him, and nothing deserves to be protected in the face of the unbridled championing of personal interests.

The Empire of Utility

This utilitarian relation to the world goes against traditional European thought. Indeed, Europeans (including the Greeks, for example) did not perceive man and the world as being disconnected from one another, viewing them instead as one single living whole. Greek man's connection with nature was not one of consumption, but of co-belonging. He did not define himself in an abstract and external way in relation to a world of objects, but in a specific manner, through the particularism of his natural and cultural belonging: his environment was thus not foreign to him, but actually defined him. He considered the world, furthermore, to be a place of divinity, a divinity that revealed its presence through a myriad of natural and artistic manifestations that bestowed upon it its very value. Within this worldview, the idea that the value of things could be primarily assessed in a subjective and utilitarian way makes no sense whatsoever, since there are neither abstract 'subjects' nor 'objects' whose existence is radically distinct and devitalised.

Historically, the first divide between man and the world to pave the way for utilitarianism appeared in the Bible, which re-organised the entire old *kosmos* in accordance with a distinction between created beings and uncreated ones. As a result of the acknowledgement of a single heavenly God, the earthly world lost its once sacred aspect. Stripped of its value, the surrounding world could thus be subdued:

> Be fruitful, and multiply, and replenish the earth, and subdue it: and have
> dominion over the fish of the sea, and over the fowl of the air, and over
> every living thing that moveth upon the earth. (Genesis 1:28)

This 'dis-enchantment' would not, however, be immediate: indeed, the mediaeval period had no notion of utilitarianism, firstly because it focused on man's relationship with God, and not on his connection to things, and secondly because it had borrowed from Antiquity the notion of a 'common good'. The almost complete devaluation of reality is actually a result of modernity, which discarded any relationship with God to overvalue individual reason (as seen with Descartes). The ideal type of utilitarian man is the *homo economicus* envisioned by economists from the 18th century onwards (even if the term itself was actually coined later) and defined as an individual whose sole purpose is to rationally maximise utility through consumption. The resulting 'empire of utility' completely eliminates all notions of beauty.

To the Greeks, the experience of beauty presupposed man's inseparability from the world. And beauty was experienced above all through sight, not intellect: one thus spoke of 'beautiful things' rather than 'beautiful ideas'. Unlike intellect, looking implies a relationship to things, a feeling of shared presence: beauty is essentially all that allows one to perceive cosmic harmony, whether in nature or art. With man defined in accordance with his belonging, experiencing beauty as harmony is what establishes his identity—none of which is possible, of course, the moment man is perceived as being separate from the world: in early biblical tradition, beauty was viewed suspiciously and often condemned (as revealed by the prohibition of all divine representations and the practice of iconoclasm) or reduced to abstraction (oriental art). In practice, however, mediaeval Christianity would blend together with European tradition and become representational. In the modern world, widespread utilitarianism is structurally incapable of envisaging any sort of harmony between man and the world, and thus lacks any notion of sheer beauty. Its awareness is limited to market prices, and everything can be sold or destroyed once a good price has been negotiated. Beauty is thus no longer, as understood by the Greeks, the very foundation of identity.

The Rise of the Bourgeoisie

Not only does utilitarianism lay our relationship with the world to waste, but it also diminishes what we are as men. Indeed, although man was traditionally defined in terms of his awareness of all that connects him to both others and his environment, his essence becomes, under the impact of modernity, one of self-consciousness. No longer primarily defined by his belonging, but by abstract individuality above all else, modern man withdraws into himself—into his interests, personal comfort and material well-being, which he sometimes terms 'happiness'. Leading a purely utilitarian life, man dries up bit by bit, gradually losing all awareness of what surrounds him, be it his own community or his natural or cultural environment. The contemporary archetype of utilitarian man is the travelling financier or consultant, whose sole purpose in life is to accumulate wealth by making beelines from airports to large hotels and back again, completely oblivious to the civilisations he's flying over and to nature itself, which he cannot see from his taxi window.

Historically, the spread of utilitarian values has gone hand in hand with the rise of the bourgeoisie. In *Der Bourgeois*,[1] Werner Sombart[2] highlights the manner in which the utilitarian mindset is born from the notion that everything can be calculated and thus de facto rationalised. The personality of the modern bourgeois contrasts with that of the mediaeval lord, whose life was fraught with prodigality, donations, unrestricted expenses, disinterestedness and a sense of honour, none of which are strictly quantifiable nor 'rational' from an individual point of view. Hence the following statement:

> To enable capitalism to flourish, natural man — i.e. impulsive man — had to disappear, as life and all of its spontaneity and originality gave way to a specifically rational mental mechanism: in short, the prerequisite for the flourishing of capitalism lay in an inversion or transmutation of all values. And it was from this very inversion, from this transmutation of values, that the artificial and ingenious being known as *homo economicus* was born.

Rather than a social class, the bourgeoisie is therefore a mentality that may well not spare anyone in its path. Sombart contrasts it with the personality of feudal or aristocratic lords. Indeed, a bourgeois is always wondering what else he can appropriate, and is enriched by what he has; a lord, by contrast, wonders what he can offer others, and is enriched by what he gives. Furthermore, whereas a bourgeois places his own interest above the community's, the opposite is true of lords. One does not, therefore, have to be rich at all to belong to the bourgeoisie — all

---

1   TN: The Bourgeois.

2   TN: Werner Sombart (1863–1941) was a German sociologist and economist.

it takes is for their sole ambition to be geared towards wealth and material comfort: a proletarian whose only purpose in life is to go on a 'low-cost' holiday to Tunisia to take some selfies amidst the palm trees is also a paragon of the bourgeois mentality. The bourgeois hierarchy places at its very top the ones who have accumulated the largest amount of money; in contrast to it, the traditional European hierarchy gives the sovereign and military functions priority over wealth alone. Obviously, these two types of mentalities have antagonistic attitudes when it comes to beauty. A bourgeois thinks to himself, 'it's expensive, so it must be beautiful', and proceeds to buy some contemporary art; for his part, a lord thinks to himself, 'it is beautiful, and therefore priceless', and goes on to contemplate the work in question. Georges Sorel[3] was thus right when he wrote that 'the sublime met its fate in the bourgeoisie'. In short, a bourgeois is incapable of experiencing the world in a poetic manner and of appreciating its beauty.

The Impasse of Utilitarianism

In terms of its perception of the world, utilitarianism displays considerable contradictions that undermine European man. First of all, an ever-growing number of works in the fields of psychology and behavioural economics have shown that the human potential to act 'rationally' is limited (Daniel Kahneman, Jon Elster, etc.). There is more, however. Having devoted all his energy to the accumulation of material goods, modern man ends up realising that his life lacks meaning: indeed, never has loneliness, suicide, and people's consumption of antidepressants and tranquilisers been so prevalent. Alone in a world of atomised individuals, utilitarian man gradually rediscovers his thirst for collective experiences and community-related thrills. Isolated in a world of commercial items, he senses intuitively that his needs are not only material in nature, but also spiritual and aesthetic. Day by day, the

---

3   TN: Georges Sorel (1847–1922) was a French political theorist, historian, and social thinker who also worked as a journalist.

world of widespread utility feels increasingly colder, impersonal, and ultimately unbearable to him.

This is by no means a coincidence: indeed, reducing all human activity to a quest for utility could never account for all social facts. In *The Sociological Tradition*, Robert Nisbet[4] clearly highlighted the extent to which the birth of sociology during the 19th century was very much a response to modern individualism. Essentially, one cannot reduce all major sociological facts to the quest for individual utility. For example, the sociological concept of 'alienation' 'is understood as a historical perspective in which man virtually becomes a stranger to himself, losing his very identity when the ties that bind him to the community are severed and he is robbed of his own moral compass'. Likewise, anthropology has clearly demonstrated that utilitarian inter-actions were rare in traditional societies. On the contrary, exchanges took place in accordance with a logic of gifts and counter-gifts (Marcel Mauss[5]). Last but not least, almost all of human history remains in-evitably incomprehensible to anyone who adopts a strictly utilitarian perspective. Just think about it: neither the placing of the Stonehenge megaliths during the Neolithic and the Bronze Age nor the construc-tion of cathedrals in mediaeval Europe make any sense to utilitarians, especially at a time when considerable resources were mobilised to build these monuments instead of being used to increase people's otherwise minimal daily comfort.

Such constructions, not to mention countless other masterpieces of civilisation, can only be understood if we acknowledge the fact that for most of his history, man did not place his own material goals above all else, but subordinated them to various spiritual and aesthetic aims.

---

4   TN: A professor at the University of California, Robert A. Nisbet (1913–1996) was an American sociologist.

5   TN: Regarded as the father of French ethnology, Marcel Mauss (1872–1950) was both an anthropologist and a sociologist.

Re-Enchanting the World

How are we, then, to escape the reign of utility? The tragedy of utilitarianism — indeed, that of individualism as well — lies in its self-fulfilling character. Modernity thus made the unfounded claim that the value of things never stretched beyond their material utility. In the name of this abstraction, many things that had hitherto been valued for their beauty, as well as their contribution to tradition and identity, were simply discarded, as they could not be justified using an acceptable cost/profit ratio. As a result, beauty, quality and disinterestedness vanished from the world to make way for sheer quantity (often of the monetary kind). Thus, all that remained over time were purely utilitarian and monetisable goods, the kind of merchandise that could be exchanged in accordance with the law of supply and demand: once a mere abstraction, utilitarianism had now become reality. Owing to this very dynamic of self-creation, it continued to gain ground, as all non-market-related aspects of our civilisational universe simply disappeared.

Although utilitarianism does, therefore, result at least in part from our own laxity, resisting it on a personal level presupposes making a conscious decision in this regard, willingly embracing the necessary efforts and discipline, and abiding by a certain attitude to life, by a certain ethical code. We must, in fact, stop thinking as individuals and, instead, think as a community. Just as we must be mindful of all that connects us with others, before taking our own individuality into account, we must also think about all that connects us with the world. For it is under this condition alone that the latter can be 're-enchanted' and its beauty restored. For this reason, we must first preserve what cannot be reduced to the level of mere merchandise, namely the cultural, natural and artistic elements that define us as a civilisation. As regards the future, it thus becomes necessary to reject the cult of material values, while giving quality priority over quantity, placing beauty above market prices, and giving birth to a new hierarchy of values. In order for us to be equal to this enormous task and provide the anti-utilitarian effort with the necessary inspiration, we will also require the presence of role models and heroes. The European civilisation abounds in them, and it is thus urgent for us to rediscover and re-interpret them.

Bibliographical References

Alain de Benoist, *Contre le libéralisme*,[6] Éditions du Rocher, 2019.

Werner Sombart, *Der Bourgeois — Zur Geistesgeschichte des modernen Wirtschaftsmenschen*, 1913. Translated from German by S. Jankélévitch as *Le bourgeois — Contribution à l'histoire morale et intellectuelle de l'homme économique moderne*,[7] Payot, Bibliothèque politique et économique, 1928.

---

6   TN: Against Liberalism.

7   TN: The Bourgeois — Contribution to the Moral and Intellectual History of Modern Economic Man.

IN PURSUANCE OF ARTISTIC RENEWAL — THE REQUIREMENT OF BEAUTY

BY ANNE-LAURE BLANC[1]

S EPTEMBER 2019: in the heart of cultural Paris, an exhibition entitled 'Rebirth(s) — Portraits and Figures of Europe' is unleashed, going against the flow — and that is an understatement. Invited by Institut Iliade, twenty artists presented and sold their works to a public that had been captivated by their talent and the sincerity of their approach. Regardless of their specific sources of inspiration and techniques, what these artists have in common is the fact that they have ventured off the beaten and accepted path: they have turned their backs on the widespread concern to keep art in compliance with power, channelling it instead towards the more adventurous tendency to embrace counter-powers. To them, no work of art will ever be a mere object of speculation. For their purpose is to make art more accessible; accessible, yet not hackneyed; accessible as a result of it being based on a long tradition that these creators have the courage to exalt without giving in to the temptation of pastiche artwork.

---

1 TN: Anne-Laure Blanc is a specialist in youth literature who also collaborates with *Éléments* magazine.

The Requirement of Beauty

Although it is hardly possible today to quickly reverse the process initiated by the deconstructors, it is in our power to at least make the salutary choice of going off the beaten track, towards an 'elsewhere' where such legacies can indeed be transcended. For the secret of art is the very secret of life. Just like life itself, it is in a state of constant renewal, accepting neither cloning nor soilless growth. Only our vitality will enable it to retain its natural centre of gravity — that of eternal becoming.

Historically, as regards France itself, the concern for beauty was once part of royal prestige: examples include Saint Louis and the building of Sainte-Chapelle and Louis XV commissioning his chief architect to design the French Military School. Such expectations would, however, come to an end in the 19th century as part of a policy of 'great works' that were both pretentious and ostentatious. The sublime thus perished with the advent of the bourgeoisie, a fact that we duly acknowledge. With the rare exception of certain city councillors turning, for instance, to Christophe Charbonnel for the creation of monumental sculptures, or entrusting old instruments to young artists, it does seem wise today not to expect too much from our politicians, just as it is preferable to forget about any private patrons, all of whom are members of the jet-set class rather than actual aesthetes. Under such circumstances, 'cultivating your own garden' in anticipation of better days is already synonymous with creating a salubrious environment. It is in this direction, an admittedly limited yet effective one, that we shall look for ways to reclaim artistic practice.

What is termed 'aesthetic' is any approach that seeks beauty, in particular (though not exclusively) by means of artistic creation and intimate contact with works of art. To clarify this statement, we shall call 'beautiful' anything that moves us, captivates us or enthuses us in an obvious yet bewildering way — for the very word 'enthusiasm' implies communion with the gods.

'The definition of the Beautiful is a simple one: *it is what makes you despair*. One must, however, praise this despair, as it undeceives you, enlightens you, and, as Corneille's old Horace used to say, *rescues you*.'

Let us leave this bittersweet definition of beauty to Paul Valéry[2] himself, a definition that he associates with the work of Stéphane Mallarmé,[3] one that is 'deeply thought-out, and the most wilful and most aware there ever was': a lucid and radiant work that contrasts with any sort of outlandish reverie.

We shall term 'beautiful' all that encourages us to admire the creative artist, whose professional prowess is often attained at the cost of long asceticism. Last but not least, let us call 'beautiful' all that creates a link between the real and the symbolic, thus allowing us to commune with the sacred; or that which forges this much needed sacredness, without which our connection with the world would be no more than pure materialism. In such a context, it is necessary to perceive art as the very creation of beauty. In addition to enabling representation, the artistic approach of Europeans is, to an equal extent, a matter of creation: it is the *poiein* of the ancient Greeks, the 'making' which, from the very outset, is sheer 'poetry'. What this approach seeks is not the 'real', but emotion, grandeur, questioning, and even inner unrest. It is indeed by venturing into the domain of 'making' that we shall be able to elude the pitfalls of wondering 'why?' and return to the firmer ground of asking 'by whom?' and 'for whom?'.

Beyond History

Indeed, to discourse on Art with a capital A would be to remain confined to a purely conceptual dimension; for as remarked by Jean-François Gautier, Art 'is combined with the other tentacles displayed by a universalising ideology that could be described as neo-Platonic,

---

2   TN: Paul Valéry (1871–1945) was a famous French poet.

3   TN: Born Étienne Mallarmé, Stéphane Mallarmé (1842–1898) was a major symbolist poet and critic.

one that is trying its hand at formulating a theory of globally valid Good, Beauty and Truth, all of which are regarded as immutable essences'. He then proceeds to remind us that 'Mnemosyne, the Hellenic goddess of "Memory", begat nine daughters known as the Muses (Calliope, Clio, Erato, Euterpe, etc.), who are still considered to be the inspirational 'advisers' of artists themselves, i.e. of all those who have mastered certain techniques, rather than advisers in the field of arts, which are but taxonomic categories, mere filing drawers'. It is therefore artists that we shall, in fact, be focusing on here.

For what are we to look for under the surface if not depth? Painting, theatre, architecture, sculpture, music, dance... For millennia, since the days when caves were first adorned with images of bison and horses, European artists have been able to give their works a plethora of shapes whose very meaning reaches beyond human history and its generations. These shapes and 'figures' have a meaning of their own and are not restricted to merely 'displaying' something. Indeed, their primary function is to evoke, symbolise and transcend all that is only partially perceived by our senses.

To the artist, it is therefore a matter of familiarising oneself with this heritage, of adopting it as one's own and being proud of it. Prior to the tourist invasion, one of the main roles of museums was to allow artists to study and imitate their elders while they completed their training in a master artist's studio. The main imperative was thus to avoid repeating long-established formulas without grasping their actual wealth, and having enriched oneself with a now internalised past, to act as a bridge between the past and the future.

And what is a talented violinist or pianist? It is a musician who, from an early age, rehearses several hours a day while studying under the guidance of a teacher. So why isn't it the same with painters and illustrators? It is, first of all, to the romantics, and secondly to the impressionists, that we owe this fantasy of the 'inspired' artist that acts as the random intermediary of a capricious or perhaps even ethereal divinity. Indeed, at the turn of the 19th century, the world witnessed a twofold movement: on the one hand, studio work began to be viewed as a numbing endeavour, even though it involved a long and demanding training which a master artist provided his companion and future disciple with. And on the other, 'academic' art, which has always been connected with the powers of official approval, lost its status in favour of self-proclaimed 'avant-garde' currents. Purchases were thus taken over by patrons and galleries, with the artist depicting himself as a solitary, poor and misunderstood individual that uses melancholy in the creation of Art. It was a cliché that truly flourished. As for the impressionists, they were, technically speaking, amateurs who, thanks to the invention of the paint tube, would complete their canvas paintings so quickly that the layers of paint, according to curators, had not even finished drying!

To complement the artist, whose work arouses emotion, one still requires the presence of a person capable of experiencing this emotion. To state things more clearly, why are we rather moved by Leonardo da Vinci's Vitruvian Man than by the elegant design of a saucepan? Rather by a symphony than by a popular tune? Rather by one of Baudelaire's poems than by a magazine article? Because we are all part of a shared history, and because our education has enabled us (or perhaps not, and therein lies the tragedy) to experience works of art since our very childhood. At times, let's face it, it is also due to a certain social conformism, to these effects of intersubjectivity that have the crowds flocking to one Parisian exhibition or another while ignoring our 'small' provincial museums, despite the fact that the latter are dominated by the kind of silence that fosters fervour, if only when one beholds a work of their choice. At other times, it is due to an immediate bedazzlement that we cannot analyse, to a sheer moment of grace that lies beyond any and all learning — which is truly a blessing.

Living as an Artist

Without further ado, we can now channel our efforts in three different directions: the safeguarding of our traditions, culture and heritage; artistic practice, even if only as an amateur; and supporting all contemporary creations 'that speak to us'.

Not a single day goes by without a church being looted, collections disunited, and books pulped. On the other hand, not a day goes by without works being reissued, paintings restored, and ancient remains exhumed. Not a day goes by without adolescents learning how to decipher oratorios and symphonies — as part of the strict study of music theory — before performing them. How long do we have left before we join the ranks of the 'outsiders' of *Fahrenheit 451*, the famous dystopia written by Ray Bradbury, who recite ad nauseam the book they have learnt by heart? It's up to us to decide. Anything is still possible, however.

How does one live their daily life 'as an artist' or remain in intimate contact with artistic creation? Although such a comparison may indeed be a bold one, why not draw inspiration from the training of athletes? One step at a time, every single day. Should you read? Yes, because literature is an art that remains accessible to us all; but why gorge on novels? A poem, a page penned by Homer, a soliloquy by one of Corneille's characters? Yes, by all means, but always mindfully. Copy them, learn them by heart, but go on stage as well — act, perform, and bring the texts to life. Should you listen to music? Yes, but not in supermarket-style, as mere background noise. Find the right position and place for genuine listening. Sing, whether alone or in a choir. Play an instrument, either by yourself or in an orchestra. All of which requires rigorous daily training, under the supervision of a teacher that assesses, advises and encourages you. Should you learn some arts and crafts? Yes, because the hand and the brain have a lot to say to one another. Because know-how is expressed in the beauty of gestures. Because crafts allow you to create, through your challenging contact with the material itself, works that 'speak' to our senses while avoiding any sort of nostalgia. Because the master-artist/student relationship lies at the very heart of transmission: luthiers, saddlers, bookbinders, glassmakers, ceramists, and cabinet-makers create a truly habitable world for us. With regard to such learning, 'fine arts' are not to be outdone. Drawing, engraving, sculpting, painting, all of it can be learnt. With humility and passion; with patience and energy.

Supporting the young European artists who embrace such an approach is a duty. Depending on our means, it might be a matter of making a purchase from them to celebrate a special occasion in our lives; of offering them a place to stay in a serene environment; or of helping them exhibit their works, perform, or record — not for the sake of their deriving mere hedonistic satisfaction from it all, but to offer them the opportunity to blossom and flourish within their own community.

Restoring today's European artists to their rightful place also implies asking them to assume their role without pretension and with a strong awareness of their mission. *Nolens volens*, we all live in a crumbling, devitalised, and anaemic age. How exacting their task is — that of familiarising us with our world and re-enchanting it! Whenever we ask them to 'entertain', it is not in view of providing us with pleasant '*amuse*ment', but of acting as our '*muse*-like' teachers that help us discover less travelled roads and shift our focus to all that is essential.

Striving for the Sacred

A work of art may also ponder the issue of our connection to time itself; our finitude, that is. Jean-François Gautier reminds us that '*Gnothi seauton*', i.e. 'know thyself', actually means 'remember that you are neither Apollo nor any other god; you are but a man, a mere mortal'. Nevertheless, 'our status is not of primary importance. Only one's manner of creating, transmitting and proliferating can shape, transfigure and elevate their existence'. It is the very intelligence displayed by our hand, and guided by instruction, that gives rise to meaning and, at times, beauty. And is it because you have cultivated your talents that you will be granted access to immortality? Very doubtful indeed… It would be tempting to believe that the path of art leads to eternity — history, however, is quick to contradict this assertion. Let us consider the example of Georges de La Tour (1593–1652), whose works were rediscovered in 1915 by the German art historian Hermann Voss; of Hieronymus Bosch, who was rediscovered by the surrealists; or the flourishing of baroque music festivals, from the second half of the 20th century onwards. Not to mention the extraordinary influence exerted by the first archaeological excavations centring around Renaissance artists, excavations that enabled ancient Greek and Roman works to once again see the light of day.

Ephemeral and unpredictable: such is the destiny of all works of art, never allowing us to forget our own mortality. And yet, we are mortals capable of being bedazzled by beauty and of striving for the sacred. As emphasised most strongly by the Spanish essayist Javier Portella, 'it is with inner agitation that we are dealing here, with the unnerving capacity to feel amazed and overwhelmed that is now lost within us. What has been left numb inside us is not our "sense of aesthetics". It is, in fact, our ability to let ourselves be carried away by the dark light of the sacred.' He then goes on to add:

> Each and every time, a statue, a painting, a poem, a symphony… will allow you to venture as close as a mortal possibly can. Yet mortal you remain: in life and in death, in light and the shadow that follows. Whenever a work drives you to stand tall, like a lord over the steep realms of truth, it ends up slipping like sand between your fingers. For it is of sand that the truth is made — such is the primary lesson that art teaches you.

And that is precisely what our artists keep pursuing and bestowing upon us: something to be shared further and with salvatory enthusiasm, for the sake of art and European culture.

Bibliographical References

Paul Valéry, *Écrits divers sur Stéphane Mallarmé*,[4] Gallimard, 1950.

Jean-François Gautier, *Peut-on être insensible à l'art?*,[5] in *Éléments*, issue number 173, August-September 2018.

Jean-François Gautier, *Peut-on vouloir être immortel?*,[6] in *Éléments*, issue number 168, October-November 2017.

Javier R. Portella, *Les Esclaves heureux de la liberté — Traité contemporain de dissidence*,[7] David Reinharc, 2012.

---

4   TN: Various Writings on Stéphane Mallarmé.

5   TN: Can One Be Insensitive to Art?

6   TN: Can One Long to Be Immortal?

7   TN: Los esclavos felices de la libertad, i.e. The Joyful Slaves of Liberty.

BEHOLDING THE WORLD'S BEAUTY — THE HORIZONS OF ADVENTUROUS HEARTS

BY PAUL ÉPARVIER[1]

'EVER SINCE the dawn of man, mankind has had but one obsession: to see what lies beyond the hill.' This is what Edmond explained to the young Marcel Pagnol[2] in *La Gloire de mon père*,[3] as the latter explored the surroundings of the family home, in the Provençal hinterland. To say that this is man's only obsession is quite a stretch. What is certain, however, is that it has characterised Europeans since the beginning of their history. Indeed, Europeans have always made a point of finding out what lies beyond the hill, sea or clouds. Whatever they snatched away from the claws of the unknown they then marked on maps, thus outlining the very borders of the world with their pencil tips. This cartography-related exploration allowed them to familiarise themselves with and understand the world around them, as did physics or philosophy in other regards. And many were the men and women of Europe who succumbed to this map madness, to this all-consuming thirst for an elsewhere: Pytheas, Erik the Red, Marco Polo, Magellan,

---

1   TN: A former scout leader, Paul Éparvier works as an executive in the private sector while also collaborating with Institut Iliade.

2   TN: The first film-maker elected to the Académie française, Marcel Pagnol (1895–1974) was also active as a playwright and novelist.

3   TN: My Father's Glory.

Christopher Columbus, Saint-Exupéry, Amundsen, Shackleton, etc. How many famous names could one still add to the list?

The landscapes of Europe themselves bear the mark of these men and their adventurous hearts: from mountain hideaways, whose remnants epitomise the conquest of the highest peaks, to the countless harbours that line our coasts and serve as gates to the seven seas; not to mention airfield runways, which act as our launch pads for sky exploration. For a long time now, the presence of the adventurous European heart has been detectable in the greater part of earth exploration, as well as in major epics and great quests. Why? Only the gods know the answer. Fame, wealth, the pursuit of dreams, the rejection of a gloomy everyday life, the thirst for discovery, and so on — indeed, there are as many reasons to seek adventure as there are adventurers.

Dirt Roads and Rocky Paths

Whether on foot, on horseback or seated in the famous two-wheeled carts that enabled Indo-Europeans to conquer the continent, adventurers began by roaming the countryside and exploring both plains and mountains to hold the unknown at bay. The countless pilgrimages that characterised the ancient world of the Middle Ages sanctified adventure along the different paths, adding a mystical, spiritual or initiatory aspect to the quest, as experienced for instance by the young Jehan in *Les étoiles de Compostelle*[4] by Henri Vincenot. Today, it is the adventurer Sylvain Tesson that praises the merits of journeying on foot. Ever dedicated to travelling across the entire world, he published, in the 2011 opinion column of *Trek* magazine, a text entitled 'I walk, therefore I am', in which he lists all the reasons that drive him to travel the world on foot or on horseback. In another of his books, titled *Petit Traité sur l'immensité du monde*,[5] Sylvain Tesson extols the *Wanderer*, the romantic traveller envisioned in 19th-century Germany, the one

---

4 TN: The Stars of Compostela.

5 TN: A Small Treatise on the World's Immensity.

who explores the forests of Europe in search of the very beauty of the world. And therein lies a very powerful aspect of one's journeying, a key source of motivation for all 'adventurous hearts': the ability to be in awe, which is neither quantifiable nor monetisable.

When it comes to major land journeys, those that take place in the mountains hold a special place of their own, because steep paths have a different appeal and require a different effort to those encountered on plains; because the risk or potential of experiencing a violent death lurks there more than anywhere else; because the views afforded to those who climb and try their hand at reflecting upon things from the mountain peak are beyond comparison. The epic adventure of Maurice Herzog, Louis Lachenal and Gaston Rébuffat, who reached the top of Mount Annapurna back in 1950, serves as the perfect summary of the very intensity that characterises a mountain adventure: the majestic and merciless peaks, the raging elements, and the men that are forced to push their physical and mental limits to the extreme. And to what end? To conquer the useless, as pointed out in a book title by the great mountaineer Lionel Terray. Therein lies, once again, one of the keys to understanding the European adventure — through the greatness of such feats, by measuring ourselves against what is greater than us.

By Sea and by Air

When one looks at the maps that Antiquity has bequeathed to us, the sea is often depicted as a frightening, disturbing and rather unknown universe. And that is probably what prompted adventurous hearts to defy it. The sea quickly became the favourite playground of European adventurers, with the Greek Pytheas departing the port of Phocaea in search of the mythical lands of Hyperborea, the Viking Erik the Red and his son Leif Erikson sailing on mere skiffs to discover Greenland and the American expanses of Newfoundland, in addition to the epics of Christopher Columbus, Magellan, James Cook and the Count of La Pérouse, all of whom were genuine lords of the seas that set off to explore the world. As regards the conquest of the sea realm, it was there that Europeans revealed to the world yet another one of their qualities: their technical brilliance. Celestial navigation, the points of sail, the shape of a ship's cutwater, rudder complexity, and various instruments enabling orientation in the open sea and in fog — so many tools that were invented, improved, and refined over the centuries to be able to venture ever further, ensuring greater safety and speed. Today, the great ocean races perpetuate this fascination, this powerful desire that drives people to face up to the elements and themselves, the sole prospect being, as with the mountaineers that emerge triumphant from their mountains, one of glory and discovery.

Having mapped the lands and the seas, Europeans devised the technological means to reach for the sky — for they longed to add a vertical axis to that of the horizons, to look at the surface that they had long travelled on foot, on horseback and by ship, but from above. This dream of flying has long been present in the European imagination. Is the tale of Icarus not among the most famous Greek myths? Beyond the tragic fate of the young Greek, who fell prey to his own hubris, one must bear in mind that it was desire to join the birds in the sky that gave his father, the architect Daedalus, the idea to construct the famous wings that would allow them to escape from the labyrinth. And it is airship pilots and aviators that are now their heirs. By taking to the skies, they gave this old dream physical shape. As for our paratroopers, '[who alternate between being eagles and lions', they would complete the cycle by connecting the heavens to the earth and giving birds legs to walk on.

The conquest of the skies also allowed adventurers to finally rise to the forefront. Although the 18th, 19th and 20th centuries witnessed the exploits of many exceptional women (the botanist Jeanne Barret, the author Isabella Bird, the mountaineer Fanny Bullock, the ethnographer Mary Kingsley, the archaeologist Gertrude Bell, the explorer Octavie Coudreau, the journalist Alexandra David-Néel, the writer Isabelle Eberhardt, and the photographer Ella Maillart, to name but a few), it was airwomen who ultimately demonstrated that, in Europe, an 'adventurous heart' could also be found among the members of the female gender. Such was, among many others, the case of Adrienne Bolland, who, in 1921, became the first woman to cross the Andes aboard a biplane made of wood and fabric, using nothing but her eyes and instinct, without any map or navigational instrument. Later on, other great female figures would also impact the history of space conquest, including the Russian Valentina Tereshkova and the French Claudie Haigneré, not to forget the Americans Sally Ride, Christa McAuliffe and Anne McClain.

The Joy of Returning to Port

Once the maps are drawn up and the territories explored, a permanent feature of the tales of European adventurers is revealed: their inexhaustible longing to return home. Tom Crean, who accompanied Robert Falcon Scott and Ernest Shackleton on three separate occasions as they attempted to reach the South Pole, thus ended up returning home to Annascaul in Ireland, where he opened an inn known as The South Pole Inn. This desire to return home is embodied most accurately by the character of Ulysses. Neither the ten years he had spent sailing across the Mediterranean nor his regular encounters with various monsters (Charybdis and Scylla) and enchanting creatures (Calypso) could ever deter him from achieving his goal — to return home and be reunited with his land, wife and son. And it is this very same mental pattern that we encounter a few millennia later with J.R.R. Tolkien and his portrayal of the Hobbits who, despite their exploits and the latter's great impact on the history of Middle Earth, never once cease to think about their beloved Shire. The author did, however, add a further aspect: that of courage, which drives Bilbo, Sam and Frodo to sacrifice their comfortable lives for a greater cause, one that they are no match for and that will enable them to grow.

The example of Ulysses — and that of many other adventurers in our European history — reminds us that it is by remaining aware of their origins, by being imbued with the very essence of their native territory, that one manages to brave the unknown and draw new maps. As stated by Sylvain Tesson in *Un été avec Homère*,[6] 'Ulysses inaugurates the dynasty of true adventurers: those who fear nothing, because they have a home port of their own. For every kingdom makes you strong'.

Awakening!

It could be said that the history of Europe is, in essence, equivalent to that of its adventurers. Indeed, it describes our periods of expansion and decline, the technological advances of our old continent and the necessary courage to experience it all. It recounts the lives of men and women who projected their dreams beyond the seas, peaks and clouds. It tells of bygone eras when Europe was great, eager to conquer and capable of self-love. Today, however, the European adventurous heart seems to be suffering from end-of-cycle syndrome. The promise of comfort and desire for material security have taken precedence over real-life risk and the desire to prove oneself in the face of one's dreams. The allure of a couch-ridden existence has prevailed over the appeal of new peaks and horizons. Europeans now live in an open world, one in which they no longer dare venture out. And yet people do travel. They have never, in fact, travelled as much as they do now, but they no longer seek adventure. Most of them are tourists, consumers of an elsewhere to which they bring their own habits — for they are as much visitors in other people's lives as they are in their own.

At times, the world does create the impression that there is nothing left for us to discover. Let us, however, change this perspective! It is time for Europe to once again heed the call of the unknown; to once again experience the thrill of uncertainty, the allure of the open sea, and the path to the summits. Let Europeans set off to rediscover their land with a desire to see what lies on the other side of the hill; with their shoes on, motorcycles whirring along side roads, and mainsails

---

6   TN: A Summer with Homer.

flapping in the cold due north wind. No, the European spirit is not dead. The outpouring of sympathy aroused by some modern-day adventurers (Sylvain Tesson, Patrice Franceschi, Nicolas Vanier, Felix Baumgartner and François Gabart, to only name a few) proves that our adventurous heart is not bereft of life, but merely dormant. Just like our very soul. And all that this adventurous heart needs is a Great Awakening that shall enable it to redraw the maps of the world.

Bibliographical References

Mike Horn, *Latitude Zero*, XO Editions, 2001.

Jean Raspail, *Septentrion*, Robert Laffont, 1979.

Saint-Loup, *Face nord*,[7] Arthaud, 1950.

Lionel Terray, *Les Conquérants de l'inutile — Des Alpes à l'Annapurna* (1961)[8] — reprinted by Paulsen Guérin, 2017.

Sylvain Tesson, *Petit traité sur l'immensité du monde*, Éditions des Équateurs, 2005.

---

7   TN: The Northern Side.

8   TN: The Conquerors of the Useless — From the Alps to Annapurna.

BEAUTY AS A PROSPECT — AN ETHICAL CODE OF CONDUCT

BY HENRI LEVAVASSEUR

T HE GREEKS described as 'beautiful and good' (*kalos kagathos*, which is the contracted form of *kalos kai agathos*) any man who manages to fully raise himself to the level of genuine human dignity. To the ancients, it was 'good' (*agathos*) to fulfil one's duties towards their city in an exemplary manner, to act and behave properly under the watchful eye of one's peers and gods, and to achieve excellence in harmony with one's nature, always reaching for the very horizons of beauty. But what is beauty? Is it only a seductive appearance, one that is fashioned by mere whim? The Greek adjective *kalos*, which is related to the Sanskrit term *kalya* (valiant), actually designates a higher form of beauty characteristic of those whose deeds bear the mark of a noble and accomplished personality. From this perspective, excellence and beauty both stem from an ethical code of conduct — a notion that lies at the very heart of European tradition and whose profound meaning is revealed by its Greek etymology.

Ethos and *Ethnos*

Contemporary dictionaries define ethics as a philosophical reflection that acts as a basis for the establishment of moral prohibitions and duties. Whereas moral prescriptions are likely to vary from one society to another, ethics are said to call for the use of reason to lay down universal principles, beyond all historical contingencies and cultural specificities. Such a notion of ethics is characteristic of the tradition of the Enlightenment and bears, of course, hardly any connection to ancient tradition.

Etymologically, ethics and morals actually refer to the very same concepts. The word 'moral' is derived from the Latin term *moralis*, which stems from *mos*, meaning 'mores', 'customs', and 'conventions': the *mos maiorum* ('ancestral custom') thus defined the morality of the Roman citizen of the classical period. As for the word 'ethics', it comes from the Greek term *ethos*, which conveys several meanings: in its first sense, the word designates the habitual abode of an animal (in Homer's writings, pastures are the *ethea* of horses). It also refers to the very dispositions of the soul, to the human character (Heraclitus teaches us that *'man's character bears the mark of divine power'*: *ethos anthropoi daimon*). Last but not least, *ethos* is used in connection with customs and mores (in his *Theogony*, Hesiod mentions the *nomoi* and *ethea* of the immortals, i.e. the laws and customs of the gods). The noun *ethos* is etymologically related to the verb *etho* (to have a custom), as is the word *ethnos* (clan, people).

These terms originate from the Indo-European root *suēdh- (to make one's own), which is encountered in the Sanskrit *svádhā* (use), the Latin *sodalis* (companion, friend) and the Old High German *sito* (custom). In the eyes of the Greeks, the word *ethos* does not therefore refer to a universal morality based on a conflict between good and evil: the notion of ethics is, instead, connected with the way one behaves when facing the world in their usual abode. The *ethos* of a people is thus rooted in tradition and based on transmission.

One also encounters this connection between the notions of custom, abode and conduct in the French terms *habitude*, *habitation*, and *habit*, all of which are related to the Latin *habitus* (way of being). Very early on, the word *habit* was associated in French with the notion of maintaining and holding, in the sense of 'maintaining one's position'. It is therefore quite fitting to speak of an ethical code of conduct, insofar as this expression allows us to delineate a type of requirement geared towards a human ideal that is characteristic of our European ingenuity. Indeed, such an ideal differs from all forms of universal morality, whose essence is either religious or secular and remains indifferent to all types of specific deep-rootedness.

An Aristocratic *Ethos*

This ethical code of conduct refers to an aristocratic ideal whose main features have maintained an astonishing sort of continuity since the days of Antiquity. Characterised by a shared kind of stoicism that is specific to all men of action, there are four fundamental types of man that have left a profound mark on the European imagination: the Homeric hero, the Roman citizen, the mediaeval knight, and the modern gentleman.

The Homeric hero is part of a world where man is assessed in accordance with the distinction between the beautiful and the ugly, the honourable and the dishonourable, and the necessity to prove oneself worthy of the respect of their peers. To the Greeks, the notion of 'good' (*agathon*) designated that which was in line with the correct arrangement of the universe (*cosmos*). The expression *kalos kagathos* applies to an ideal of human perfection in which the quality of appearance coincides with that of being. And it is education (*paideia*) that aims to achieve this harmony between the body and the soul; between thought, word and action. Conversely, any manifestation of excessiveness (*hybris*), both among men and gods, results in disaster. This is in sharp contrast with Western modernity and its metaphysics of the unlimited, which Heidegger denounced — the desire to 'always have more', which must be countered with a logic of the 'always better'.

Heir to the Greek world, the Roman civilisation also bequeathed to us an aristocratic ideal of great value: that of the citizen of the classical era. The latter comes across as being constantly concerned about his personal and familial *dignitas*, which must be defended at all times, even at the cost of his own life. Indeed, *dignitas* is rooted in *virtus*, a quality that is specific to man (*vir*): fortitude and self-control (*gravitas*) thus lie at the very core of Stoic teachings. These qualities are inseparable from the notion of *pietas*, that is to say from the duty owed to both the gods and one's family, in addition to the duty to serve the state. One of the members of the Scipio family thus had the following words engraved upon his tomb:

> By my character I added to the acts of courage (*uirtutes*) of my family. I begat offspring, I emulated the deeds of my father. I maintained the praise of my ancestors so that they rejoice I was born from their line. Honour has ennobled my stock.

Mediaeval chivalry adopted a part of this heritage, which it combined with both Christian virtues and the old martial ideal of Celtic and Germanic societies. In his *Histoire et tradition des Européens*,[1] Dominique Venner states that it is an 'incarnate ethical code': 'Prowess, generosity and loyalty are those of its attributes that honour sums up. The elegance of the soul commands one to be valiant to the point of recklessness'.

The requirement to remain true to one's word forces a man to stand by his oath to the death, an attitude that is exalted in the *Nibelungenlied*. The ideal of heroic sacrifice, present throughout the epic tradition, mingles with a Christian message in the Saxon poem *Heliand*, which depicts Christ and his disciples as a Germanic prince and his vassals, with the wedding of Cana coming across as a feast of warriors.

In modern times, the figure of the gentleman embodies the synthesis and culmination of these various legacies, establishing a balance between the abilities of the swordsman and those of the man of wit, thus combining moral elegance, refinement, courage and self-control. This is the ideal that is generally shared by all European elites and

---

1   TN: European History and Tradition.

which the Prussian *Junker* and the British *gentleman*, for instance, strive to embody.

Embodying the Ethical Code of Conduct

What specific lessons can our European youth still learn from these examples, which are so far removed from our daily reality? Aren't these models now outdated? The truth is that although the aristocratic ideal has not actually disappeared, it no longer shapes our society; the dominant values are, instead, those of hedonism and egalitarianism. The very notion of elite has, to a large extent, been stripped of its value, provided, of course, that it is not associated with human types that are entirely different from those of the ancient aristocracy. Mediocrity and vulgarity are now met with unprecedented complacency. A genuine inversion of ethical and aesthetic principles has imposed itself upon the masses, masses that are overwhelmed by mass recreation and relentless advertising.

And yet each one of us can still choose to embody a part of the European ethical code by implementing it — on both a feminine and masculine level — in a variety of situations and undertakings. This possible line of action thus takes on a scope that reaches far beyond mere individual destinies. Indeed, this ethical code of conduct acts as a perfect means to bring about a genuine community-related reform of both minds and behaviours, a prelude to the indispensable awakening of our dormant Europe. It is a path of excellence which our European youth must, once again, learn to take.

Although it may seem difficult to specify the objective criteria of such 'conduct', everyone has the ability to instinctively determine what should be rejected, namely neglect, vulgarity, and laxity. The latter can, in fact, take various shapes: body-related laxity (neglectful weakening or boastful displaying), garment-related laxity (universal and unisex clothes), behavioural laxity (having no self-control, disregarding the rules of courtesy), language-related laxity (excess or vulgarity), mental laxity (intellectual laziness, conformism), and character-related laxity (loss of one's sense of honour, courage deficiency, lack of commitment to one's principles).

We must therefore counter all these forms of self-neglect with the notion of exceptional conduct, one that represents a kind of asceticism. This does not, however, imply leading an ascetic life: indeed, beyond its religious meaning, which found its way into Christian terminology via the Christian Latin term *asceta*, the word is related to the Greek term *askesis* (exercise), which originally referred to the practice of a type of artistic or athletic activity. Asceticism is thus, above all, synonymous with discipline. The above-mentioned ethical code of conduct is ultimately rooted in one's desire to live the European way, in accordance with the triad of Homeric principles: to have nature as one's foundation, excellence as one's goal, and beauty as one's prospect.

Giving Shape to One's Existence

To acknowledge nature as one's foundation is to respect the natural order of things and the major sources of its ecological and anthropological equilibrium; to preserve and transmit the specific characteristics of our European genetic inheritance; and to immerse ourselves in the splendour of our landscapes and remain committed to the community-related aspects of our traditions through the celebration of the traditional festivals that punctuate each annual cycle.

To define the quest for excellence as one's goal is to maintain one's concern for moral elegance while simultaneously exercising a certain restraint and having high expectations of oneself. It is to strive for harmony of thought and action, of being and appearance, while always aiming to surpass oneself rather than seek some kind o hedonistic 'fulfilment'. It is to submit to willingly consented discipline rather than advocate total freedom; to be aware that one is but a 'link in a long chain', to serve others rather than oneself; to be demanding in one's choice of peers while remaining capable of enduring loneliness. Last but not least, it is to pass on these requirements to others by setting an example, never denying oneself in the interest of ease, comfort or security. The surest way to achieve this purpose is to build one's 'inner citadel' not only through daily meditation and reading, but also through physical discipline.

To choose beauty as one's prospect is never to let hideousness and unseemliness take over, making sure that one evades their grasp as much as at all possible. It is to take advantage of every opportunity to feed one's soul and mind by contemplating beauty and perceiving it as a manifestation of the sacred. It is, furthermore, to express this concern for beauty and elegance to the best of one's ability, right down to the smallest details of one's everyday life, including the objects that surround us, the adornment of our living space and our dress code — all in accordance with our European sense of aesthetics. This is indeed the surest way to illuminate, awaken and transmit. For this ethical code of conduct is also a type of aesthetics: to abide by it is thus to give shape to one's very existence.

Bibliographical References

Dominique Venner, *Histoire et tradition des Européens — 30 000 ans d'identité*, Éditions du Rocher, 2002.

Dominique Venner, *Un samouraï d'Occident — Le bréviaire des insoumis*, Pierre-Guillaume de Roux, 2013.

CONCLUSION

IT IS WHEN THE LIGHTS GO OUT THAT THE TORCHES MUST BE LIT!

BY GRÉGOIRE GAMBIER[1]

EVEN IN THE darkest night, glimmers of light still subsist, like traces of the day that often defy explanation. Are these beams remnants of a bygone age, akin to stars that died thousands of years ago yet continue to shine as a result of their distance, singing their own 'stellar swansong'? Or is it already a new break of day that now heralds its presence in the very depths of darkness? In all likelihood, the answer lies, once again, in our ability to look past the duality of opposites... There is thus but one certainty: one must favour the ceaselessly renewed light of breaking dawns to the false promises of a great revolution. As stated by José Antonio, 'our place is outside, though we may occasionally have to pass a few transient minutes within. Our place is in the fresh air, under the cloudless heavens, weapons in our hands, with the stars above us. Let the others go on with their merrymaking. We, outside in tense, fervent and certain vigilance, already feel the dawn breaking in the joy of our hearts'.

---

1   TN: Grégoire Gambier is a French journalist with a degree in history.

Standing Tall in the Face of the Gathering Dusk

There is a civilisation seemingly doomed to fade away, to gradually be erased from the map of physical, biological and mental representations: our European one. And yet, how are we to live if not in the hope that the essential will endure? Are we already dead, only existing thanks to the inertial force of time and space, and the weight of history and memory, akin to the last gleams of a star long since dead? Or are we merely at a crossroads once more, defying our very destiny and faced with the choice of life or death, which we 'old Europeans' have always borne within ourselves? Renaud Camus[2] writes:

> As the world that I have loved so much crumbles further, its last remnants seem all the more beautiful to me: the skies, the trees, the faces, the grammar, the politeness, the dogs, the blossoming cherry tree amidst a still leafless thicket, and every gentle and kind gesture.

And it's at this time of confusion, when the temptation to embrace nostalgia afflicts even the stoutest hearts, that Institut Iliade has chosen to take up its struggle, specifically in order to evade the incapacitating nostalgia that is so characteristic of all 'conservatives' and that ushers whole generations of activists towards a dead-end — at a time when, having come out of the last European civil war, we have continued to face the emergence and accumulation of many perils that require our civilisation to espouse a new kind of 'grammar'.

The onset of decadence is manifested through a feeling of defeat, a feeling internalised to the point of rendering unbearable the 'white man's burden' that Kipling had already glorified. The logical consequence is self-abandonment, renunciation, dishonour and ultimately death. Having lowered our gaze, we would then throw up our hands in despair. Prior to accepting the Great Replacement, we would thus accept the Great Erasure by renouncing all that defines us. We would

---

2   TN: Renaud Camus is a French writer who came up with the notion of the 'Great Replacement'.

start by kneeling down and end up presenting our very necks, as we are ultimately beheaded by our executioners, whose eagerness to indulge in massacre would thus obviously increase tenfold.

The Algerian War Has Not Yet Ended

In his works, ranging from *L'Art français de la guerre*[3] (which was awarded the Goncourt Prize in 2011) to *Féroces infirmes*[4] (2019), Alexis Jenni uses a novelist's flair to describe the scars left by a nameless war whose traumatic impact continues to gnaw away at our society. Indeed, there was a time, not so long ago, when Europeans paid a dire price for the mere fact of being European — and this happened in departments that were actually French and protected by French law, i.e. in ones that had their own prefects, police force, teachers and newspapers. At the time, French people of European descent — or 'FSE's, according to the official terminology — went from being 'settlers' to becoming targets, not to say prey. All in the space of barely a few years. The balance of power was thus irremediably reversed, with the 'dominant' becoming the 'dominated'. The Oran massacre, perpetrated on 5 July 1962 (i.e. more than three months after the official end of the hostilities) in one of the most powerful bastions of the last supporters of a French Algeria, marked the conflict's climax: 'FSE's were tracked, hunted down in the streets and bled like animals. As for the exact figures, they have been the subject of much debate. Whereas Guillaume Zeller estimates that nearly seven hundred Europeans fell prey to FLN killers, other sources report that the dead and the missing were as many as 3000. Regardless, this leaves us with one basic reality: a specifically ethnic hatred aroused by the mere fact of being 'European'. Admittedly, many Muslims also paid a heavy price for their attachment to what they believed to be France; but the impulse to indulge in pogroms, one of the vilest tendencies of man (who does not suffer from any lack in

---

3   TN: The French Art of War.

4   TN: The Ferocious Infirm.

this regard), impacted 'FSE's in particular. This tendency is what we witnessed in Oran (1962), but previously also in Sétif on 8 May 1945, not to forget the small mining village of El Halia, near Philippeville, where seventy-one European men, women, children, old people and infants were suddenly attacked and massacred in 1955 by their own Muslim neighbours, under particularly gruesome circumstances. Just like 'a revolution is not a dinner party' (Mao Zedong), the war in Algeria is not a novel: it is the harsh reality of what can happen to a people left to its own fate, one that mistakenly believes that the army, i.e. the institutions, will ensure its protection.

And yet there is another, deeper explanation for this abandonment policy: *self*-abandonment. If, at the time, the regime was able to impose its decisions, it was first and foremost by pandering to the weariness of a people that could no longer bear the few sacrifices required by its past greatness (a 'small war' right outside its own borders), because its dreams were limited to the establishment of the consumer society heralded by the Glorious Thirty, the Americanisation of its mores, the lust for comfort that always precedes the worst kind of conformity, and the dissolution of one's being in the abyss of ownership and outer appearances ... Dominique Venner was right when pointing out the fact that the 'policy' adopted at the time was very short-sighted indeed (though he was not alone to do so): by giving up on having any sentries at the *limes* of the empire, it is one's own 'inner empire' (Alain de Benoist, 1995) that one ends up renouncing. 'And each sentinel among men is responsible for the whole of the empire', Antoine de Saint-Exupéry once pointed out. Although inevitable, France's departure from Algeria should have taken place under honourable circumstances. And it was our honour, the most precious asset of all, that was sacrificed on African soil.

The result of this deliberately hedonistic headlong rush, of this slow plunge into 'the icy waters of egotistical calculation' (Karl Marx), was evidenced by the events of May 1968, by the downfall of our traditional society and ancient rural anthropology, and by the use of labour immigration to 'exploit' others, ultimately culminating in mass-scale immigration, increasingly overt Islamisation, vociferous 'indigenous' resentment, and low-intensity terrorism (as attested by the widespread outbreak of street criminality), which, although resulting undoubtedly from foreign invasion, are above all symptoms of the prior relinquishment of our will to remain ourselves.

A Call for Renewed Resistance

Such relinquishment, however, is now out of the question. In a book that focuses, among other things, on his experience of the Algerian war, Dominique Venner concludes that 'every man bears within himself a tradition that makes him what he is. And it is up to him to discover it. Tradition is a choice, a whisper of both ancient times and the future. It tells me who I am. It tells me that I come from somewhere.' It is towards this rediscovery, this return to our perennial sources, that Institut Iliade channels its efforts. Ever radical, its contributors tackle the very roots of the evils that gnaw away at today's Europe, with the following certainty acting as their guiding star: 'An abyss is what separates us from those who strive for material well-being'.

Instead of the horizontal and non-hierarchical organisation of needs, impulses and rights, the authors of Institut Iliade propose an alternative in which 'nature', 'excellence' and 'beauty' are finally assigned the task of nourishing the soul, releasing it from its torpidity and elevating it. To live, to love, to experience, to fight, to serve, and to transmit: what emerges from these contributions is a thirst for rediscovered freedom; a desire to embrace one's own fighting spirit and community; and a taste for ceaselessly renewed adventure — all of which are characteristic of every people in human history.

Threatened with potential disappearance, our ancient civilisation may seem to be facing its own twilight. Such a situation, however, is not unprecedented in our European history, on the tortuous path of our 'long memory'. It would be tempting to compare, as David Engels[5] invites us to do, our situation with the fall of the Roman Empire, perhaps even with the collapse of the Roman Republic, which paved the way for the rise of the Empire. Another analogy is also possible, with all the reservations that the very thought brings: the long 'autumn of the Middle Ages' — an era characterised by the chaos of political conflicts and social reconstitutions from which new forms of organisation, i.e. modern states, will emerge; by the repercussions of the great plague and particularly an obsession with death that shall lead to new religious practices centred around the salvation of the soul; and, above all, by a rediscovery of Antiquity, by a return to one's roots, an endeavour that is always essential when, in times of crisis, one is required to 'think and act' to safeguard their future. All, of course, in intimate intertwining with the past, but with the necessary energy to only keep the latter's best aspects. As flawlessly explained by Johan Huizinga,[6] the society of the Middle Ages had to die in order to give birth to another, that of the Renaissance, thus opening a new chapter in our history. For there is always a green twig that sprouts from the trunk of our old Europe.

For a New European Rebirth

It is thus definitely by becoming ourselves again, by reaching into the depths and thousand facets of all that makes up our European identity, our specific (and not 'universal') way of existing in the world, that we shall be able to open up, by means of a Great Return to our roots, new possibilities for all future Europeans, for the generations born during and for the storm, thus engendering a new and fierce kind of enthusiasm: that of destiny. Here is what Ernst von Salomon[7] states in

---

5   TN: David Engels is a historian who also acts as Chair for Roman History at the University of Brussels (ULB).

6   TN: Johan Huizinga (1872–1945) was a Dutch historian who contributed to the founding of modern cultural history.

7   TN: Ernst von Salomon (1902–1972) was a German screenwriter, novelist and Weimar-era national revolutionary activist.

The Outlaws: 'We are not fighting to make the nation happy—we are fighting to force it to tread in the path of its destiny'.

As we now enter the '20s of a new century, this book can still be paraphrased and avail us. For as long as Europe 'burns dimly in some daring minds', it can continue to exist, 'shining radiantly where those imbued with its spirit dare[d] to expend even their last efforts for its sake'.

What this means is that it will once again be necessary to show courage, as our friend François Bousquet[8] urges us to do in his 'cultural guerrilla handbook'. Perhaps even heroism, in our Spengler-like awareness that heroism is not only a matter of facing up to one's 'specific enemies', but also (and maybe above all) one of enduring certain 'states of the mind', realizing, just like Evola, that to embrace one's heroic purpose is 'to face the most swirling wave, knowing that two possible fates await us at equal distance: the fate of those that shall end with the dissolution of the modern world, and that of those who will find themselves on the central and royal axis of the new current'.

The old world is dead... So what? Every twilight demands that we envisage, *hic et nunc*, the breaking of new dawns, that we rebuild the foundations of a genuine 'common home' for our peoples and nations, and that we undertake alternative, mobilising and (owing to their very fruitfulness) potentially victorious ventures. Indeed, this is what Institut Iliade essentially suggest we do.

In this regard, the necessary condition is for every European to henceforth consider himself a rebel endowed with the qualities described by Jünger in his famous 10th treatise: the refusal to allow the powers-that-be to impose their rules upon us, regardless of 'whether they use propaganda or violence', while remaining 'determined to defend oneself'. The spirit of resistance, i.e. that of 'reaction', is thus both the prerequisite and the fuel of any 'revolution'.

---

8   TN: Born in 1968, François Bousquet is a French journalist, editor and essayist.

A new revolution, you say? Oh, we're prepared for it. Better yet: we long for it, and have every intention to bring it to life, at the very moment when many historical cycles and ideologies are running out of breath and coming to a close, which is particularly true of the mercantile, individualistic and 'liberal' modernity imposed by the Enlightenment.

The night is complicit and propitious. New torches are already being lit, which is but one of the many signs of the awakening and rallying of our younger European generations.

May this work act as a fire ship.

Bibliographical References

Renaud Camus, Twitter, 5 February 2020.

Guillaume Zeller, *Oran, 5 juillet 1962 — Un massacre oublié,*[9] Tallandier, collection Texto xxème, 2012.

Dominique Venner, *Le Cœur rebelle,*[10] 1994. New edition by Pierre-Guillaume de Roux, 2014.

Ernst Jünger, *Das Wäldchen 125 — Eine Chronik aus den Grabenkämpfen,* 1925.[11] Translated from German by J. Hervier as *Le Boqueteau 125.* New edition by Christian Bourgois, 2000.

David Engels, *Le Déclin — La crise de l'Union européenne et la chute de la république romaine — Analogies historiques.*[12] L'Artilleur, 2013.

Johan Huizinga, *Herfsttij der middeleeuwen,*[13] 1919. Translated from Dutch by J. Bastin as *L'Automne du Moyen Âge.* Payot, collection Petite Bibliothèque Payot, 1995.

Ernst von Salomon, *Die Geächteten,*[14] 1930. Translated from German by A. Vaillant et J. Kuckenburg as *Les Réprouvés.* New edition by Bartillat, collection Omnia poche, 2016.

---

9   TN: Oran, 5 July 1962 — A Forgotten Massacre.

10   TN: The Rebel Heart.

11   TN: Copse 125: A Chronicle from the Trench Warfare of 1918.

12   TN: The Decline — The EU Crisis and the Fall of the Roman Republic: Historical Analogies.

13   TN: Autumn of the Middle Ages.

14   TN: The Outlaws.

François Bousquet, *Courage! — Manuel de guérilla culturelle*,[15] La Nouvelle Librairie, 2019.

Oswald Spengler, *Écrits historiques et philosophiques — Pensées*,[16] Copernic, collection Or du Rhin, 1980.

Julius Evola, *Rivolta contro il mondo moderno*,[17] 1934. Translated from Italian by P. Baillet as *Révolte contre le monde moderne*. L'Âge d'Homme — Guy Trédaniel, collection Delphica, 2009.

Ernst Jünger, *Der Waldgänger*,[18] 1951. Translated into French by H. Plard as *Traité du rebelle ou le recours aux forêts*. New edition by Seuil, collection Points Essais, 1986.

---

15 TN: Courage! Cultural Guerrilla Handbook.

16 TN: Historical and Philosophical Writings — Thoughts.

17 TN: Revolt against the Modern World.

18 TN: The Forest Passage.

STYLE AND CONDUCT

BY ALAIN DE BENOIST

I HAVE BEEN asked by Institut Iliade to reproduce, at the end of this book, an article that I had originally published in *Le Figaro* on 14 October 1978 under the title 'Yes, style maketh man'. The French phrase itself stems from a passage taken from a speech delivered by the famous naturalist Georges-Louis Leclerc de Buffon at the *Académie française* on 25 August 1753. As for its focus, it related to the style of writers: 'Style is man himself'. What Buffon meant by this is that the way in which one expresses themselves in words involves and simultaneosuly reveals all the faculties that are specific to man. In other words, it is the form, if you will, that always reveals the core. And it was only afterwards that the expression acquired a more general meaning.

Style then came to be seen as being more or less equivalent to conduct: there are thus some that are endowed with style, and others that are not.

When re-reading the last lines of this text, which was published a long time ago, I cannot, of course, help thinking of Dominique Venner who, just like the prefect Spendius de Montherlant, also chose to embrace a voluntary death. I think of him all the more because Dominique was the very model of proper conduct. Dominique Venner's 'testament', that is to say his posthumous book, is entitled *A Samurai of the West*. It is difficult to approach this 'breviary of the rebellious' as one would approach other books, especially when one reads the following sentence in it: 'Only a suffered death has no meaning. When intentional, it has the meaning one gives it, even when it remains devoid of practical utility'. Or this one:

> It is here and now that our fate plays out. And this final second is as important as the rest of a lifetime — which is why one must remain themselves until the very last moment. Especially at the very last moment. For it is by deciding for oneself, by truly longing for one's destiny that one can vanquish nothingness.

Reading these words, it is hard not to feel one's hands tremble.

At the time when my style-related article appeared in *Le Figaro*, I had already published in the July issue of *Item* magazine an article that would subsequently be reprinted in *Les Idées à l'endroit* (1979) under the title 'The Twenty-Five Principles of "Morality"'. My use of quotation marks around the word 'morality' meant that I was not referring to the kind of morality that relates to sin, but to the ethics of honour. I shall now include a summary of this very text.

1. The body and the soul are one and the same.

2. It is not enough to be born; one must also be 'created'. This creation takes place after one's birth, for one can only be 'created' by themselves. And that is how we give ourselves a soul. Meister Eckhart[1] thus speaks of 'self-creation' (*Selbstschöpfung*): 'I was my own cause. [...] Then it was my Self I wanted and nothing else. What I wanted I was, and what I was I wanted'.

    A similar logic is encountered in the Eddas (*Havamal*, V), where Odin sacrifices himself to himself. Likewise, peoples found their own culture the moment they become their own cause, when they derive from within themselves (from their own tradition) the source of their own perpetual renewal.

---

1   TN: Meister Eckhart was a Catholic theologian, philosopher and mystic.

3. Virtue is not a means to some ultimate end. For it is an end in itself, acting as its own reward. One must thus reclaim what lies within; one must reclaim themselves — for such is the starting point of any quest or conquest. To impose a sovereign empire upon oneself. To simultaneously obey the Master and command the Slave that lurk within us.

4. Being oneself is not enough. For one must become what one can be, shaping oneself in accordance with his self-perception. Never be satisfied with yourself. Long to change yourself before wanting to change the world. Accept the world as it is rather than accepting yourself as you are. Develop, within yourself, those potentialities which make you specifically human; and among them, those that make you specifically yourself. And begin by cultivating your inner energy, the energy that 'an ant can summon up as much as an elephant can' (Stendhal) and which allows one to be all that, in times of winter, allows spring to return.

5. Set your own standards — and stick to them. Abide by your own law and never yield nor submit. Persevere without having any reasons to. Be faithful to causes others have betrayed; be loyal for those who have not been so. Furthermore, be faithful to those who no longer are. Defend, both against everyone else and yourself, the perception you have of things, as well as the one you would like to have of yourself.

6. Only take 'control' of others once you have taken 'control' of yourself: indeed, placing constraints upon oneself is the first requisite for the right to impose some on others. The demands that a great man makes are on himself; those of a petty man are on others (Confucius). Power must be founded on superiority, and not superiority on power. Those who rule have the right to possess, but those who possess do not necessarily have the right to rule. A man of quality is beyond despotisms: for he dominates the dominators using his own means. The higher you climb, the

more you walk alone; and the more you have to rely on yourself. Those who are above are responsible for those below: they must thus meet their expectations — should they fail to do so, all revolts are justified. Willingly follow those who are superior to you: take pride in having found a Master (Stefan George). The counterpart of submission is not domination, but protection. We have the right to obey and the duty to command (ourselves) — not the other way around. Proclaim the duty to have rights, as well as the beautiful right to have duties.

7. Every existence and self-assertion is tragic — and so is all of history. All that occurs has no other meaning than the one we bestow upon it. On the other hand, everything impacts everything else: our tiniest actions thus have consequences even in the most remote parts of the universe.

8. Do not merely accept, but desire what is happening; desire it whenever you have failed to prevent it from occurring. Instead of resignation, embrace attitudes that allow you to maintain your own freedom. *Amor fati*: such is the only course of action when all courses of actions have failed. Make sure that what you cannot impact in any way has no impact on you either.

9. In the beginning was the Act (Goethe). There is no reason for great and powerful actions; and that is why such feats must be performed. The action is what matters most, not the one that makes it happen; the mission is important, not the one who accomplishes it. Stand against individualism, ever in favour of active impersonality. Indeed, what must be done cannot be understood on the basis of motives. For nobility speaks through action.

10. Honour: never fall short of the standards that you have set for yourself. For the image that we have of ourselves is realised the moment we conform to it on a permanent basis. Thus, whether it is an 'image' or a 'reality' ceases to matter, as the two terms

become indistinguishable. The idea is thus made flesh: such is the true incarnation of the *Logos*. Every promise is binding, and no circumstance could ever undo this. Your ability to be proud of yourself is the best way not to have to be ashamed of others.

11. Style maketh man. For liturgy matters more than dogma. Beauty is never an evil, and the beautiful is always real. Indeed, it is preferable to do well in mediocre undertakings than badly in great ones. The way we do things matters more than the things themselves. The manner in which one implements his ideas is more important than the ideas themselves. The way one lives is worth more than what one experiences in his life — and sometimes even more than life itself. If a man has more simplicity than manners, he is a lout; more manners than simplicity, a prig; endowed with both simplicity and manners — such is the superior man (Confucius).

12. Nietzsche: 'What is noble?' To seek out situations that require elevation, leaving happiness and comfort to the masses. To strive to be, rather than to appear. To have the ability to make enemies everywhere and, at the worst, to proceed to make one of oneself.

13. To give duty priority over passion, and passion priority over self-interest. Performing 'good deeds' to earn one's salvation is still synonymous with serving one's own interests. Do what you must, not what you love. This, however, requires some learning: indeed, remaining ever mouldable, man needs rules to shape himself. Let your work, therefore, be a service, and your duty your destiny.

14. Achieve and constantly redefine the true harmony that results from contingencies and principles. Make sure that your actions match your words. For a man whose words exceed his deeds is no more master of himself than a man whose actions go beyond his very words. Sincerity is thus not synonymous with telling the truth. To be sincere is actually to completely adhere to everything that one undertakes, without having any ulterior motives.

15. Do not repent, but learn your lessons. Take all possible steps to avoid causing harm. Should harm still result, avoid justifying your actions. Indeed, the justifications that one tends to give himself are but his attempts at self-evasion. The purpose of repentance is not to erase one's mistake, but to ease one's own conscience. Return good for good, and justice for evil.

16. Never forgive, but forget a lot. Never hate, but despise often. There are many base feelings, including hatred, resentfulness, touchiness, vanity, and greed — with hatred being the opposite of contempt, resentment the opposite of forgetting, touchiness and vanity the opposite of pride, and greed the opposite of wealth. Of all these feelings, it is resentment that is the most contemptible. Nietzsche states: 'Alas, the time of the most despicable man is coming, he that is no longer able to despise himself'.

17. Stand against utilitarianism. What applies to armies applies to men as well: any troops that need to know why they are fighting in order to fight properly are mediocre troops to begin with. And there is worse: troops that need to be convinced that their cause is a good one. And worse still: those who only fight when they stand a chance of winning. Whenever you have to undertake something, keep all your concerns about the endeavour's success secondary. The principle of taciturnity remains key to understanding Dürer's famous engraving, *Knight, Death and the Devil*. It is, however, not enough to undertake things without being sure of one's success; indeed, it is also necessary to make endeavours even when you are certain to fail, as faithfulness to one's own standards is the only honourable way to proceed. Think of the 'soldier of Pompeii' described by Spengler, and also of the example set by Marcus Atilius Regulus. To want to imitate one's adversary under the pretext that he was successful is to become that adversary and not to differ from him. Baseness emerges as soon as one asks himself 'what for?', 'what do I stand to gain?' and

'why must I do this?'. Striving to preserve at all costs a life that one is bound to eventually lose is utterly absurd.

18. Both virtue and vice can only be the prerogative of an elite group, as they require the same capacity for self-control. One's freedom to do something must always go hand in hand with one's freedom *from* it. In other words, one must only want what one feels he can forgo.

19. Do not seek to convince, but rather to awaken. For life finds its meaning in what is more than life. And what is more than life is not expressed in (and through) words, but sometimes felt. Give precedence to the soul over the spirit, to life over reason, and to image over concept.

20. Lyricism and poetry can act as one's 'moral' principles provided that one has defined man's relation to the universe, and not his relation to his fellow man, as the essential relation of their very existence. Great heads of state are those thanks to whom peoples can have a lyrical perception of themselves, retaining a poetical existence from their own perspective.

21. The present realises all pasts and potentiates all futures. To accept the present through one's joyous embracement of the moment is to be able to enjoy every moment simultaneously (*carpe diem*). Past, present and future are the three equally actual perspectives specific to any moment of historical becoming. One must, once and for all, break with the linear conception of history, for all that we do involves what has already come to pass and what is yet to come (back).

22. The purpose of life is to place something of importance between oneself and death.

23. Loneliness — knowing how to be akin to the North Star, to the one that remains in place when all others continue to spin. Stillness is at the centre of movement (Jünger) — in the axis of the wheel.

Cultivate within yourself that which a man of quality preserves, ever immutable, under all circumstances: the inner core of his being.

24. The only genuine piety is filial piety, one that is extended to include one's ancestors, lineage and people. Our dead ancestors are not spiritually deceased, nor have they moved on to a different world. They remain by our side, as part of an invisible and whispering crowd. As long as we perpetuate their memory, we, their descendants, will continue to be surrounded by them. And that is what justifies our ancestor cult and our duty to have their names respected.

25. All men of quality are brothers, regardless of race, country and period.

I could now add many other principles to those listed above, which were formulated quite a while ago; perhaps even correct some of them — but that is a different story.

L'INSTITUT ILIADE FOR LONG EUROPEAN MEMORY

L'Institut Iliade for Long European Memory, based in France, was born from an observation. Europe is but a shadow of her former self. Replaced by outsiders, confused by having lost their bearing and their pride, Europeans have abandoned the reins of their common destiny to people other than themselves. Europeans no longer remember. Why? Because amongst the current elite — whether at school, university, or in the media — no one passes down to them the cultural wealth of which they are the inheritors.

Contrary to this moribund current, L'Institut Iliade has given itself the task of participating in the renewal of the cultural grandeur of Europe and in aiding Europeans' reappropriation of their own identity. Facing the Great Erasure of culture, we intend to work for the Great Awakening of European consciousness and to help prepare Europe for a new renaissance — one of identity, freedom, and power.

L'Institut Iliade's calling is threefold:

- To train young men and young women concerned about their history to always build. To make them the avantgarde of the renaissance for which the Institut calls: men and women capable of giving to civic and political action that cultural and metapolitical dimension which is indispensable. Their motto: to put themselves at the service of a community of destiny, which risks disappearing if it is not taken in hand. Armed with a strong culture relating to European traditions and values, they learn to discern that the adventure that awaits them entails risks and self-sacrifice, but also enthusiasm and joy.

- To promote a radical and alternative vision of the world contrary to the dogmas of universalism, egalitarianism, and 'diversity'. Using all available means, the Institut develops concepts and ammunition to understand and fight the modern world.

- To gather together, especially — but not only — in France, those who refuse to submit and who are inspired daily by the Homeric triad as described by Dominique Venner: nature as the base, excellence as the goal, beauty as the horizon.

L'Institut Iliade's originality, especially with the aim of reformulating and updating knowledge, lies in tying together the seriousness of its content with ease of learning for the greater public, the objective being to demonstrate an authentic pedagogy, and to act in complementary or supportive ways with other initiatives having the same goal.

L'Institut Iliade's action takes place across various channels:

- A cadre school of the European Rebirth, which every year brings together trainees from a wide variety of backgrounds and is already seeing citizens from other European countries participate;

- an annual colloquium — made up of academics, politicians, writers, journalists, and association officials from all over Europe — that meets in Paris to discuss strong and challenging themes, such as 'The Aesthetic Universe of Europeans', 'Facing the Migratory Assault', 'Transmit or Disappear', 'Nature as Base — for an Ecology of Place', 'Beyond the Market — Economy at the Service of Peoples';

- the publication of works — designed as beacons to enlighten readers' thoughts and guide them toward the reconquest of their identity — within several collections, made available in the widest array of languages and European countries;

- artistic exhibitions on the fringes of contemporary artistic trends, allowing the public to take a fresh look at art and rooted creation;

- an incubator for ideas, businesses, and associations to support and help the greatest number of projects — with quality and sustainability criteria — across all fields of civil society (culture, commerce, etc.) that seek to impose a rooted vision of the world and an alternative to the current system, while prioritising structures and projects making an impact in real life;

- an active presence on social media, allowing us to reach new audiences (through videos, publications, annual events, and news presentations), centred around a website that functions as much as a resource hub as it does as a platform for exchanges and debate, notably offering an ideal library of more than five hundred works, a European primer, a dictionary of quotations, and turnkey itineraries for visiting and hiking the prominent places of European memory.

Education through history:

L'Institut Iliade endeavours to uphold in every circumstance the richness and singularity of our heritage in order to draw forth the source and the resources of a serene, but determined, affirmation of our identity, both national and European. In line with the thought and deeds of Dominique Venner, the Institut accords in all its activities an essential place to history, both as a matrix of deep meditation on the future as well as a place of the unexpected, where anything is possible.

CONCERNING EUROPE, it seems as though we will be forced to rise up and face immense challenges and fearsome catastrophes even beyond those posed by immigration. These hardships will present the opportunity for both a rebirth and a rediscovery of ourselves. I believe in those qualities that are specific to the European people, qualities currently in a state of dormancy. I believe in our active individuality, our inventiveness, and in the awakening of our energy. This awakening will undoubtedly come. When? I do not know, but I am positive that it will take place.

— DOMINIQUE VENNER, *The Shock of History*
Arktos Media, London, 2015

Follow L'Institut Iliade at
www.institut-iliade.com
linktr.ee/InstitutILIADE

OTHER BOOKS PUBLISHED BY ARKTOS

OTHER BOOKS PUBLISHED BY ARKTOS

GUILLAUME FAYE	*Archeofuturism*
	Archeofuturism 2.0
	The Colonisation of Europe
	Convergence of Catastrophes
	Ethnic Apocalypse
	A Global Coup
	Prelude to War
	Sex and Deviance
	Understanding Islam
	Why We Fight
DANIEL S. FORREST	*Suprahumanism*
ANDREW FRASER	*Dissident Dispatches*
	Reinventing Aristocracy in the Age of Woke Capital
	The WASP Question
GÉNÉRATION IDENTITAIRE	*We are Generation Identity*
PETER GOODCHILD	*The Taxi Driver from Baghdad*
	The Western Path
PAUL GOTTFRIED	*War and Democracy*
PETR HAMPL	*Breached Enclosure*
PORUS HOMI HAVEWALA	*The Saga of the Aryan Race*
LARS HOLGER HOLM	*Hiding in Broad Daylight*
	Homo Maximus
	Incidents of Travel in Latin America
	The Owls of Afrasiab
RICHARD HOUCK	*Liberalism Unmasked*
A. J. ILLINGWORTH	*Political Justice*
ALEXANDER JACOB	*De Naturae Natura*
JASON REZA JORJANI	*Artemis Unveiled*
	Closer Encounters
	Faustian Futurist
	Iranian Leviathan
	Lovers of Sophia
	Novel Folklore
	Prometheism
	Promethean Pirate
	Prometheus and Atlas
	Psychotron
	Uber Man
	World State of Emergency
HENRIK JONASSON	*Sigmund*
EDGAR JULIUS JUNG	*The Significance of the German Revolution*
RUUBEN KAALEP & AUGUST MEISTER	*Rebirth of Europe*
RODERICK KAINE	*Smart and SeXy*
PETER KING	*Here and Now*
	Keeping Things Close
	On Modern Manners

OTHER BOOKS PUBLISHED BY ARKTOS

OTHER BOOKS PUBLISHED BY ARKTOS

ERNST VON SALOMON	*It Cannot Be Stormed*
	The Outlaws
WERNER SOMBART	*Traders and Heroes*
PIERO SAN GIORGIO	*CBRN*
	Giuseppe
	Survive the Economic Collapse
SRI SRI RAVI SHANKAR	*Celebrating Silence*
	Know Your Child
	Management Mantras
	Patanjali Yoga Sutras
	Secrets of Relationships
GEORGE T. SHAW (ED.)	*A Fair Hearing*
FENEK SOLÈRE	*Kraal*
	Reconquista
OSWALD SPENGLER	*The Decline of the West*
	Man and Technics
RICHARD STOREY	*The Uniqueness of Western Law*
TOMISLAV SUNIC	*Against Democracy and Equality*
	Homo Americanus
	Postmortem Report
	Titans are in Town
ASKR SVARTE	*Gods in the Abyss*
HANS-JÜRGEN SYBERBERG	*On the Fortunes and Misfortunes*
	of Art in Post-War Germany
ABIR TAHA	*Defining Terrorism*
	The Epic of Arya (2nd ed.)
	Nietzsche's Coming God, or the
	Redemption of the Divine
	Verses of Light
JEAN THIRIART	*Europe: An Empire of 400 Million*
BAL GANGADHAR TILAK	*The Arctic Home in the Vedas*
DOMINIQUE VENNER	*For a Positive Critique*
	The Shock of History
HANS VOGEL	*How Europe Became American*
MARKUS WILLINGER	*A Europe of Nations*
	Generation Identity
ALEXANDER WOLFHEZE	*Alba Rosa*
	Rupes Nigra

Made in the USA
Middletown, DE
20 May 2024